Identifying & Enhancing
the Strengths of
Gifted Learners
K–8

Identifying & Enhancing the Strengths of Gifted Learners

K–8

Easy-to-Use
Activities
and Lessons

Ann Maccagnano

CORWIN PRESS
A SAGE Publications Company
Thousand Oaks, CA 91320

For information:

Corwin Press
A SAGE Publications Company
2455 Teller Road
Thousand Oaks, California 91320
www.corwinpress.com

SAGE Publications Ltd.
1 Oliver's Yard
55 City Road
London EC1Y 1SP
United Kingdom

SAGE Publications India Pvt. Ltd.
B 1/I 1 Mohan Cooperative Industrial Area
Mathura Road, New Delhi 110 044
India

SAGE Publications Asia-Pacific Pte. Ltd.
33 Pekin Street #02-01
Far East Square
Singapore 048763

Printed in the United States of America

Library of Congress Cataloging-in-Publication Data

Maccagnano, Ann.
Identifying and enhancing the strengths of gifted learners,
K–8: Easy-to-use activities and lessons / Ann Maccagnano.
        p. cm.
Includes bibliographical references.
ISBN-13: 978-1-4129-5198-2 (cloth)
ISBN-13: 978-1-4129-4253-9 (pbk.)
    1. Gifted children—Education (Elementary) 2. Education, Elementary—
Activity programs. 3. Lesson planning. I. Title.

LC3993.22.M32 2007
371.95′72—dc22

                                        2006102702

This book is printed on acid-free paper.

07   08   09   10   11   12   10   9   8   7   6   5   4   3   2   1

Acquisitions Editor:	Stacy Wagner
Editorial Assistant:	Joanna Coelho
Production Editor:	Denise Santoyo
Copy Editor:	Kris Bergstad
Typesetter:	C&M Digitals (P) Ltd.
Cover Designer:	Lisa Miller

Contents

Acknowledgments

Thank you to my husband, Anthony, who convinced me to write this book. He has been very supportive throughout my whole educational experience.

Also, special thanks to my friend and mentor, Patricia Weber, for starting me on this journey in gifted education.

Thanks also to developmental editor, Katie Jones, for guiding and assisting me through this endeavor.

Corwin Press would like to thank the following reviewers for their editorial insight and guidance:

Frank Buck, PhD, Curriculum Supervisor
Talladega City Schools, Talladega, Alabama

April DeGennaro, Teacher, Gifted K–5
Peeples Elementary School, Peachtree City, Georgia

Sheila Eller, Elementary Principal
Mahtomedi Public Schools, Mahtomedi, Minnesota

Debbie Jo Halcomb, Fourth Grade Teacher
Robert W. Combs Elementary School, Happy, Kentucky

Raynice Jean-Sigur, PhD, Assistant Professor of Early Childhood
    Education
Kennesaw State University, Kennesaw, Georgia

Mary Johnstone, Principal
Rabbit Creek Elementary School, Anchorage, Alaska

Ken Klopack, Art & Gifted Education Consultant
Chicago Public Schools, Chicago, Illinois

Kathy Lineberger, School Library Media Coordinator,
former third-grade teacher of academically gifted students
Marvin Ward Elementary School, Winston-Salem, North Carolina

Kathie F. Nunley, Educational Psychologist,
Developer of Layered Curriculum(R)
Brains.org, Amherst, New Hampshire

Peggy Rogers, First Grade Teacher
Burton Elementary, Rexburg, Idaho

Joan Franklin Smutny, Director of the Center for Gifted
National-Louis University, Skokie, Illinois

Sharon Weber, Principal
Punxsutawney Area School District, Bell Township Elementary,
    Mapleview Elementary, & Mary A. Wilson Elementary Schools
Punxsutawney, Pennsylvania

About the Author

 **Ann Maccagnano** is a Gifted and Talented Specialist in the Kenmore Town of Tonawanda School District in Tonawanda, New York. She has a Master's Degree in Elementary Education with a Gifted Education Extension Certificate and has received the Outstanding Undergraduate in Elementary Education (OUEE) Finalist Award. She has been teaching gifted students for the past eleven years. She is married and has two wonderful daughters.

1

Developing and Nurturing Gifted Students' Strengths

There is nothing more unequal than the equal treatment of unequal people.

Thomas Jefferson

Every classroom has children with a wide range of abilities. As the teacher, As the teacher, you are responsible for acknowledging and fulfilling the special needs of each child, but recognizing individual needs is not always an easy task—some children show their talents outwardly, but others are often quiet observers. It can be even more difficult to identify gifted children: standardized testing can aid teachers in determining those who have a high intellectual potential, but these tests do not always provide information concerning the creative and affective domains that frequently affect a child's success in developing talented behaviors.

As a teacher of gifted and talented children for more than eleven years, I now know that each gifted child is different in his or her own way; all gifted children have unique abilities that must be understood and addressed. These students bring their own interests, observations, knowledge, and talents to the classroom. Our challenge as educators is to recognize and encourage these qualities so that our students learn something new every day.

■ THE CHALLENGE OF CHALLENGING CURRICULUM

Children who are gifted learn content easily; these children need novel and challenging curriculum to reach their potential. C. June Maker and Aleene B. Nielson (1995) note in their book, *Teaching Models in Education of the Gifted,* "Since gifted students can acquire information more rapidly and almost effortlessly, they should apply it in new situations, use it to develop new ideas, evaluate its appropriateness, and use it to develop new products" (p. 5). They need *challenging* work, not just more work. Open-ended questions, guided discovery, complex abstract ideas, problem solving, freedom of choice, higher-level thinking skills, and creativity are important components for a quality education for gifted students (Maker and Nielson, 1995) and need to be properly addressed for school success.

Addressing Both Weaknesses and Strengths

Another problem compounds the difficulties of providing the right lessons for students: a child who is labeled "gifted" is not necessarily gifted in all areas. Some children excel in math while they struggle in language arts. Take, for example, Paul, one of my students.

Paul

When I first met Paul, I asked him his name and he didn't reply—thankfully, his friend told me his name! After talking with his regular classroom teacher, I found out that Paul didn't like to talk or share many of his ideas in class, but his teacher said that he loved math. In fact, Paul excelled in mathematics well beyond his grade level. He could do calculations in his head very quickly and accurately, solve complex math problems effortlessly, and see patterns easily using his visual/spatial intelligence. Yet when I gave Paul a language arts task, he struggled to accomplish it. He was all about the numbers.

Teachers need to realize that gifted students may not excel in all areas; on the other hand, these children do have great potential in certain subjects and it is important to provide them with experiences to strengthen this potential. The key is to challenge the students in a way that helps them grow to be more well-rounded.

Children like Paul need be challenged in their area of strength. I wanted Paul to grow in math while also trying to strengthen his area of weakness, his communication skills. To do this, I asked him to share with the rest of the class how he solved a particular math problem. Explaining math problems was engaging to him and also strengthened his weaker areas. I believe encouraging gifted children in all curricular areas will assist them in the future. In my experience, these children want to take risks and pursue their interests, and thrive on being challenged in and outside the classroom.

WHAT THIS BOOK OFFERS   ■

This book is designed to help K–8 teachers identify a student's areas of potential giftedness and provide appropriate activities and units of study to develop and nurture these talents to their fullest. The earlier we can identify children's strengths, the better we, as educators, can guide their learning. When gifted students learn early on that they can receive good grades for applying little effort on a project, they conclude that being smart means doing things easily. Then when these students are presented with a complex task, they have a hard time tackling the challenge and becoming a risk-taker. Also, gifted students may think school is boring and lose interest in learning if they are not challenged in their school career.

Identifying giftedness in children can sometimes be a difficult task because many classroom teachers may not know the characteristics to look for. In addition, sometimes children are not considered gifted because of what the teacher views as their inappropriate or unacceptable behavior within the classroom. They may often disagree and argue their point of view with others; they are not interested in details; they may hand in messy or careless work; they refuse to accept authority, tend to be bossy, and dominate group situations, discussions, or others; and they can become bored easily with routine tasks, which causes misbehavior and daydreaming. It is my hope that you will see these characteristics as evidence of a gifted child, not of a troublemaker who needs to be punished.

Spotting a child's giftedness through regular observations is very important, especially because not all forms of talents are easily testable. For example, creative students may be overlooked because most standardized tests do not test for creativity. With this knowledge in mind, teachers can use this book as an informal guide for assessing students' gifted potential. This book should not replace formal testing; it should be used in conjunction with a variety of measures. Remember, the key to identification is regular observation—trust your own judgment if you feel a student shows gifted tendencies.

I have written this book to help provide challenging and engaging lessons and activities to stimulate gifted children. These activities offer immediate informal assessment of students' strengths and needs in the cognitive, affective, and creative areas, which can assist in planning programs and learning experiences that will better awaken their unique talents. In addition to developing your students' abilities, the analysis activities can also be used as extension and enrichment of your everyday curriculum. The units of study and activities are intended to motivate, excite, and entice students to learn more in their area of strength.

HOW THE BOOK IS ORGANIZED   ■

The book is broken down into the following categories: language arts, creative thinking, critical thinking, interpersonal and intrapersonal intelligence, mathematical ability, and visual/spatial awareness. Each chapter begins with informal activities that I call "analysis activities." I use the term *analysis* because the activities are not outright tests; they are tools to help you uncover the skills and talents that children in your classroom have.

Teacher notes and grading guides are listed, and following the analysis activities are lessons, activities, and units of study to use with students who excel in the subject. Also within each section I have listed characteristics that are common in students gifted in the subject. Some of these characteristics are similar in many of the areas. Several of the lessons can be placed into a few of the chapters, but I placed them where I thought that they would best tie into the curricular area.

Many of the projects that are in this book help gifted children use and develop their creativity in different ways. Paul Torrance (1979), a pioneering researcher who studied creative thinking, describes the four components of creativity as fluency, flexibility, elaboration, and originality, categories that are still used today. Fluency pertains to generating as many ideas as possible to open-ended questions. Flexibility is looking at ideas in different ways or from different perspectives, whereas elaboration is embellishing or adding to an idea. Originality is having unique ideas and developing them. It is important to incorporate all of these components in order to establish and strengthen creativity within the classroom, especially to ensure that creative thinkers develop their gifts.

■ USING ANALYSIS ACTIVITIES

Assessing a student's strengths is essential to providing him or her with the appropriate curriculum. The informal analysis activities, which are presented at the beginning of each section, can be used by the classroom teacher or the gifted-and-talented teacher to gauge the student's area of strength. These collections of activities and games offer the teacher tools with diagnostic and teaching potential. Administering these activities to small groups of students or individually is recommended. Best of all, these activities are ready to use and only limited materials are required.

By administering the activities, you can obtain important information about your students and their strengths, which can be put into their permanent folders to show their growth throughout the years. Please remember that the results of the analysis activities should be used as a guide to help discover the strengths of students, not a cutoff mark for being gifted or not-gifted.

Selecting and Administering the Activities

Select the activities that you want your students to complete. Keep in mind that it's not necessary for all students to complete all of the analysis activities. Choose from the activities in each target area and select those that are appropriate for the student. If you don't know where the student's strengths lie, administer all of the activities that you feel may be *appropriate* for that student. But if you know that the child excels in mathematics, there's no need for her to do the math analyses because you already know where her strength lies. Don't waste your time or the students' by administrating the analysis activities in their known strength area. The lesson ideas within the section that follows will provide useful and challenging learning experiences for that student—without the unnecessary testing.

Although it's possible to administer many of these analyses out loud, I suggest that you copy those activities you will use on colored paper for durability and make an additional copy of the activities so that anecdotal notes relative to the students' responses can be taken. Some activities do not need to be duplicated. Guidelines and suggested instructions are provided for each activity; a minimal amount of extra supplies will be needed, such as drawing materials or a set of pentominoes.

Grading

After administering the analysis activities, refer to the Teacher's Notes for acceptable answers. Some activities have no one correct answer; however, a wide variety of creative answers will show that students are strong in that particular area. When you are done critiquing the activities, gather all the activity notes together and place them in the student's folder. These activities should provide a better understanding of the student's needs and talents, which then can be addressed with the appropriate learning opportunities. Please remember that these are informal analysis assessment tools and should not be used to exclude someone from a gifted program. There is no cutoff score for each analysis activity that indicates whether a student is gifted or non-gifted. The activities were developed to show where students' strengths lie and then provide challenging ideas and units of study for those students to extend their learning.

WHAT TO DO AFTER AREAS OF ■
STRENGTH ARE IDENTIFIED

After administering the activities and discovering a student's strength, what do you do next? The sections following the analyses are designed to provide engaging activities and units of study to enhance and broaden learning experiences. Keep this book handy throughout the year to add a spark to curriculum learning, engage learners, and help students grow in their area of strength—you'll notice that your students will have a positive attitude toward school and be more productive in their own learning.

As noted researchers Caine and Caine (1991) put it, "Brain research establishes and confirms that multiple complex and concrete experiences are essential for meaningful learning and teaching" (p. 5). Once you know the subject in which the student should be challenged, it is easy to provide the proper activities to accelerate that student's educational growth.

Novelty has been shown to be a very important component in the successful education of gifted students, and novelty is what this book hopes to provide. Teachers of gifted students need to get the students' curiosity engaged so they maintain a love of learning instead of losing it. Gardner (1991) states, "It is effective to use subject matter that can be related to the students' own lives and to engage students in activities affording them the opportunity to take a hand at various roles" (p. 237). The activities in this book encourage the use of technology, role-playing, and community service, all of which enable students to see how the subject matter can be used in their everyday lives.

The lessons in the book can be used with individuals, small groups, or the entire class, as you see fit. For example, some of the lessons in the creativity section can be used with the whole class—everyone is creative and lessons on how to enhance and develop these skills will benefit all of your students. Other units, however, will not be appropriate for the whole class because of the challenging content level. I have found that grouping gifted students together by interest level or area of strength is the best possible scenario for them when tackling a challenge. Gifted children feel more comfortable showing and sharing their strengths with children who think like they do. "Gifted students can better understand and accept their learning difference if there are others just like them in the class" (Winebrenner & Devlin, 1996, p. 1). When students are grouped together based on a topic of interest, they become highly motivated and excited about their own learning (Reed & Westberg, 2003). It should also be noted that many gifted children like to work alone on projects, so I also give them a chance to work independently.

Delving into new, appropriate enrichment experiences will lead our brains to grow and change (D'Arcangelo, 1998). Teachers also need to design learning around students' interests, immersing them in complex, interactive experiences that provide real, meaningful challenges for them. I make a point of presenting lessons that are very different from the regular curriculum, which piques students' interest and motivates them to learn something new. Students that I've worked with can't wait to tackle these new problems, and now your students can be just as excited!

2

Language Arts

Language arts, or the skills needed to communicate, is an essential component of our society. Some children can communicate better than others, either orally or through writing, because they have a natural gift in this area.

Some characteristics that are common among gifted individuals with language arts strengths include:

- Possessing a storehouse of information about a variety of topics
- Having an unusually advanced vocabulary for their age
- Recalling information quickly and accurately
- Being intense when truly involved in an activity
- Questioning everything; favorite question is "Why?"; having an argumentative nature
- Displaying original thinking
- Being highly verbal
- Having a great imagination; being a daydreamer
- Liking to read, talk, tell stories, word games, and listening to stories or to other people talk
- Enjoying language, word play, and verbal communication
- Having unique ideas in their writing and speaking
- Using drama and humor to engage an audience in imaginative ways through their writing or drama experiences

By working on enhancing communication skills, students benefit from an increased ability to express themselves in all avenues of their learning. Some children, however, demonstrate giftedness in the language arts and should receive special attention, like Alexis.

> **Alexis**
>
> A fifth-grade teacher approached me about a student she had who wrote phenomenal poetry but who was not in my gifted class. The teacher asked if I could give Alexis an opportunity to join the other gifted students during my poetry unit. I read some of her work and was flabbergasted by her use of words and creative details, and how easily her poetry seemed to flow. She really was a gifted poet. When she joined the class for my poetry unit, I made sure that I provided challenges and avenues that would help expand her linguistic strengths. I introduced her to different poetry styles to help broaden her knowledge. After studying Shakespearean sonnets, she wrote her own sonnet in iambic pentameter, just like Shakespeare. She loved having this opportunity to share and utilize her strength in poetry. Alexis excelled in my class and was fortunate to have had a teacher who recognized her needs and provided her with an opportunity to further improve her strengths in the language arts.

The following activities are designed to assess how well students use verbal and written communication skills. Fluency, the attention to detail, the ability to ask appropriate questions, spelling, and grammar are important aspects that are addressed. For younger students, of course, spelling and grammar aren't relevant, as most do not read or write; check instead for fluency in their verbal responses.

■ ANALYSIS ACTIVITIES

Activity 1: Verbal Sequencing

Teacher Notes/Grading: This activity is designed to check for verbal skills, fluency, and elaboration as students give the correct sequence of events for certain experiences.

Children who communicate effectively will give very detailed answers to questions. They will elaborate on each aspect of the process that they go through without repeating themselves or going back and saying that they forgot something.

Following is a good sample response for how to make a sandwich. You will notice the underlined sections are very detailed aspects of the answer. These specific details do not have to be included in a response, but are offered because they are examples of exceptionally well-crafted answers. Remember to look for unique details and proper sequencing of events.

> First, I would take out a plate <u>from the cupboard and place it on the counter.</u> Then I would go over to the breadbox and take <u>two slices of wheat bread out of the bag</u> and place them on the plate. <u>Opening up the refrigerator,</u> I would take out a slice of cheese, the ham, and the mustard. I would then take <u>the wrapper off</u> the cheese and place the cheese on the bread. Then I would place a slice of ham on top of the cheese and then <u>squirt</u> some mustard on the ham. After <u>placing the other slice of bread on top</u> of the mustard, I would <u>take a knife from the drawer and cut the sandwich in half. That is how to</u>

<u>make a ham and cheese sandwich. All you need to do is eat it. Don't forget to clean up by putting the mustard away, throwing the cheese wrapper in the garbage, and washing the plate.</u>

Directions:

a. Tell how you make a sandwich.

b. Tell how you play a game.

c. Tell how you make a bed.

d. Tell how you get ready for school.

Activity 2: Written Communication

Teacher Notes/Grading: Students may choose a topic to write on one or you can choose the topic for them. Check for grammar, spelling, punctuation, fluency, and elaboration in the student's writing piece.

Children who write effectively will give you very detailed answers. Good responses will include specific details, original ideas or thoughts, and correct spelling and grammar.

Directions:

a. Write a letter to a child in another country.

b. What would you tell a famous person if you could meet him or her?

c. If you were an eraser, what would you say to the child using you?

Activity 3: Mystery Box

Teacher Notes/Grading: Place a single object in a box. By asking questions, students should try to determine what is in the box. Remind them that they can ask detailed questions, like Twenty Questions. Look for good verbal skills and creativity in their thinking. Instead of just asking "Is it a penny?" children should try to ask more questions about categories, such as "Is it round?" or "Is it found in the playground?" to help narrow down the choices. This shows their creative thinking. Just because they don't guess correctly doesn't mean that they are not gifted in this area. You should look for good thought processes, not just correct guesses.

Activity 4: Book Writing

Teacher Notes/Grading: Check for detailed writing, clarity of ideas, spelling, and grammar. A good answer to this activity includes complete thoughts and original ideas incorporated into the writing.

Directions:

What type of book would you write? Explain why.

■ ENHANCING READING AND WRITING SKILLS

Being able to successfully communicate ideas in written form or orally is a talent. Providing engaging opportunities for students who excel in the linguistic area is necessary for them to continue to reach their fullest potential as learners.

Listed in the following section are language arts units and activities that I have found to be very motivating to children in my classroom. They include reading, writing, debates, discussion groups, book clubs, plays or skits, mock trials, and speeches. I suggest that you select the activities that would best fit each child or group of students.

Greek Mythology Unit

Myths are stories that try to explain natural phenomena. My students really enjoyed studying Greek mythology. I have never seen my fourth graders so excited about learning! They just loved reading the stories and were productive during class periods. After reading several myths, they selected the project they wanted to do to present what they had learned. The project options and requirements were:

Become a Greek God or Goddess. Research a god or goddess and become that god or goddess by acting like him or her. Develop an oral presentation telling facts about your Greek god or goddess. The other students will try to guess who you are, so remember not to tell anyone! Include another interesting piece to this project, such as designing Poseidon's trident or Pandora's box.

Create a Board Game. Research and come up with a board game all about Greek mythology. Be sure to create questions, a game board, directions on how to play the game, and game pieces. This game will be played and shared with the whole class.

Create a Newspaper. Create a newspaper about the everyday happenings of the Greek gods and goddesses. It should include various articles, advertisements, and even comics. The use of creative ideas is very important.

Create Your Own Greek God or Goddess and Myth. Create your own god or goddess and create a myth around him or her. Remember to include detailed descriptions and personal characteristics of your god or goddess.

My students loved these projects because they had options for displaying their own learning. I have found that creating choices for the students increases their motivation to learn. Author Steven Levy (1996) proposes that learning is more meaningful when students select the topic for a project than when teachers assign the work.

Cosmic Comic Writing

Studying and creating comic strips are a great way to motivate students to use their imagination while learning character development, using inferential skills, and utilizing literary devices like point of view. I like to start this unit by having students brainstorm a list of comics that they are familiar with, which incorporates the fluency component of creativity. Then as a class, students use the flexibility component of creativity by placing the comics into categories. Sharing a variety of different styles of comic strips, such as the "funnies," political comics, graphic novels, and superhero comics, is very important to show different writing styles. Have students bring in their favorite comic to share with the class. Using the different types of comics, students should analyze each comic's characters, use of dialogue, genre, message, and progression from one frame to the next.

How a comic strip is set up is significant. Be sure to point out the different types of frames that are used to enhance or draw attention to the frame and the use of language. The critical aspect that I share with my students is that you don't have to be an artist to create a comic—what is important is that the ideas are there.

After students have the background knowledge on comics, they can develop their own comic. Comic strip topics may include creating a new superhero that helps solve a real-world problem, such as recycling or endangered species, or creating a political cartoon that deals with a community issue.

Comics Resource

National Association of Comics Art Educators, www.teachingcomics.org

Poetry

"Poetry presents an opportunity for gifted students to explore (1) the quality of words, (2) the power of metaphoric language, and (3) the complexity and subtlety of meaning" (Smutny, 2001, p. 1). Creating an atmosphere where poetry is shared, appreciated, and understood is very important. The study of poetry is not just about learning the different styles of poetry. Reading poetry for pure enjoyment is a very beneficial learning process for all ages. "Poetry has the power to help children distill their deepest perceptions and thoughts: it also acts as a springboard to other creative work" (Smutny, Walker, & Meckstroth, 1997, p. 92).

Introducing poetry to students should be done in such a way that it can be applied to real-life experiences. Providing these experiences will lead students to be more motivated, sense a purpose for learning poetry, and enjoy learning about it. For example, if the class reads poems about nature, it's beneficial to go outside and read these poems again, outside "in nature." Students will probably look at the trees and plants from a different point of view. Filling the classroom with a wide variety of styles of poetry for students to read is also very important.

After the students have a good grasp of the meanings and feelings that poems share, they can start to write their own. Gardner (1983) states, "The young poet generally begins his self-education by reading other poets and by imitating their voices as best he can" (p. 82). Once they are more confident, they should be able to find their own voice. An author's personal voice is what gives the writing personality and its unique style. Voice is one component of the six writing traits created by the Northwest Regional Educational Laboratory to help teachers guide writing instruction ("6 + 1

Trait Writing," 2005). The other traits are ideas, organization, word choice, conventions, and sentence fluency.

Limericks

A limerick is a five-line funny poem, in which lines one, two, and five rhyme and lines three and four rhyme. After teaching the class about limericks, I combine the concepts and rules of limericks and math together. I have students create number limerick poems for others to solve (see example below). Students should first read a variety of limericks to get a sense of the rhythm and rhyme of this style. Then they select a number and write clues to describe the number in a limerick. Problem-solving skills and creativity are blended together to solve these puzzles. Stephan Krensky's (2004) book *There Once Was a Very Odd School and Other Lunch-Box Limericks* is a wonderful resource on limericks.

Number Limerick Example:

I am a two-digit prime,

Whose digits add up to a dime.

The largest digit you see,

Is a multiple of three,

I hope you find me out in time.

Answer: 19

Sharing Poetry

Ideas for sharing original poems or students' favorite poetry include:

- Creating a poetry journal or diary with illustrations
- Creating a poetry slideshow on the computer, incorporating sound, video, and pictures
- Reciting poetry in a circle, such as an author-sharing chair or book talk
- Planning a night of poetry sharing with family and friends through a Poetry Talk
- Incorporating poetry in drama experience
- Creating an anthology of students' poetry

Personification

Personification is a way of giving inanimate objects or ideas human characteristics, feelings, or actions. I like to read various personification poems to students for them to get a feel for that style. To practice personification, students can select an object and personify it either in a sentence or as a monologue. For example, the wind is personified in the sentence, "The wind felt tired of pushing the leaves around in the street." To culminate the personification activity, I give the students a piece of paper with random lines and a shape on it. Students incorporate these lines and shapes into a picture. Using the personification poetry tool, students then personify their picture with a poem. This activity incorporates the creativity components of elaboration and originality.

Poetry and Drama

Mixing poetry and drama together by acting out original published poems or even poems that students have written makes learning more meaningful and authentic. Acting out poetry improves communication skills, social skills, cooperative learning skills, and memorization skills, and provides for a deeper understanding of poetry. The rules for Poetry Drama are:

- Students form groups of two or three to act out a poem.
- Students must work collaboratively to break the poem down into speaking and acting parts.
- Students may not use any props.
- Students must memorize the poem that they are acting out.

After students have rehearsed their poems, I invite parents, teachers, and students to the auditorium for their presentation of "Partying With Poetry." The students love bringing poetry to life, and this also gives the audience a different avenue from which to view poetry.

This idea came from a workshop that I attended called Poetry Alive. For more information, see the Poetry Alive! Web site at www.poetryalive .com. Students can even submit their own original poems for a chance to be selected for the Poem of the Month on this Web site; it also lists great Web sites where students can play with poetry online (click on the "Resources for Students" links).

Poetry Web Sites

Giggle Poetry, www.gigglepoetry.com

Poetry4Kids, www.poetry4kids.com

Teaching Poetry Web Sites

Favorite Poem Project, www.favoritepoem.org/

Tips for Teaching Poetry, www.inspiringteachers.com/tips/curriculum/ poetry.html

Fables and Folktales

Everyone is familiar with fables and folktales. Talented students can delve deeper into a unit on fables and folktales by looking for the morals or important parts of the story, while developing and writing their own fable or folktale.

Fables are short stories in which animals are the characters. These animals have human characteristics and solve a problem, teaching the reader a moral. Teaching the class about Aesop and his fables is a good starting point. Folktales are stories that have been passed on orally from generation to generation. They usually begin with "Once upon a time . . ." and describe human nature or how things came to be. Activities that can be done with fables and folktales include:

- Guess-the-Moral Game: After the teacher reads a fable, students guess the moral of the story; points can be awarded.
- Students write and illustrate their own versions of fables or folktales.
- Create a moral match sheet: list the morals of several fables and have students find which fable correlates with each one.
- Create puppets and produce a puppet show of a particular fable.
- Create a skit from a folktale to share with others.
- Create a diorama or visual representation of the major parts and characters of the folktale.

Fable Web Sites

Aesop's Fables, www.umass.edu/aesop/fables.php

Page by Page Books: Aesop's Fables, www.pagebypagebooks.com/Aesop/Aesops_Fables

StoryTymes Aesop's Fables, www.childclassics.com

Fables and Folktale Drama

Infusing drama into this unit by putting on fable or folktale plays will motivate students. Two books, *Aesop's Fables Plays for Young Children* by Dr. Albert Cullum (1993) and *Folk Tale Plays From Around the World—That Kids Will Love!* by Marci Appelbaum and Jeff Catanese (2001), include plays for students to act out. These drama-learning experiences don't need to be elaborate with detailed costumes or props. I have students create simple masks out of foam board for props to create a quick and easy play.

Folktale Problems to Solve

The book *Stories to Solve: Folktales From Around the World* by George Shannon (1985) and its sequel (Shannon, 1994) contain folktales with a problem-solving twist. I usually read one of these short folktales to the class once a week. My students love trying to find the solution to the folktale. This is a great critical-thinking and higher-level thinking activity.

Free Writing

Writing comes in various forms, from creative writing to informational writing. Many talented writers don't like to be restricted to a particular topic, so I allow students time to free-write on a topic of their choice, which improves their motivation. An independent study project lends itself to gifted writers by giving them the time and freedom to write for enjoyment. If you'd like your class to write on the same topic, use any of the following creative-writing prompts:

What if all clocks stopped?

What if your parents went away on a permanent vacation and left you in charge?

What if money really did grow on trees?

What if you never grew up?

What if everyone had two heads?

What if animals could talk?

What if you were a pencil? Describe your adventures.

What if it was your birthday every day of the year?

What if you could invite anyone from history to a dinner party? Who would it be? What questions would you ask?

Word Play

Palindromes, transmogrifications, and anagrams can be used as word-play activities that are entertaining, challenging, and enhance vocabulary. Following are some ideas for playing with words.

Palindromes

Palindromes are words, phrases, sentences, or numbers that read the same forward and backward. Some palindrome examples are dad, mom, wow, racecar, and stop pots. Activities using palindromes can include:

- Students create a list of all the palindromes they can think of. This develops the fluency component of creativity.
- Students create a palindrome puzzle book that gives hints to a particular palindrome, such as "What is a three-letter palindrome for a loud sharp noise?" (pop). This develops the originality and elaboration components of creativity.
- Students create phrase palindromes with illustrations. This also develops the originality and elaboration components of creativity.

Palindrome Resources

Too Hot to Hoot: Funny Palindrome Riddles, by Marvin Terban (1985)

Transmogrification of Words

Transmogrification is the act of changing into a different form or appearance. I have students use the dictionary or thesaurus to change simple sentences or phrases into complex language or vice versa. For example, the phrase "The grass is always greener on the other side" can be changed to, "The lawn is constantly emerald in the opposite section." Try changing the following well-known book titles or phrases into transmogrifications:

The three little pigs

Sample Answer: The trio of diminutive swine

The farmer in the dell

Sample Answer: The cultivator in the glade

Good night, sleep tight

Sample Answer: Pleasant hours of darkness, slumber taut

For a culminating activity, students create their own transmogrifications of famous quotes, nursery rhymes, or book titles. Their final product can be put into a booklet or on a poster that includes illustrations and an answer key.

Anagrams

An anagram is a word made by using the letters of another word in a different order. The only rule is that every letter must be used in the new word or phrase. This unit of study will have students use their creative and critical-thinking skills in order to make an anagram. One example of this is the word "step," which can be made into the word "pets." Students can create an anagram challenge puzzle book with answer key for others to solve. This activity can be done independently when they have extra time. A nice Web site on anagrams is www.many things.org/anagrams/.

Root Words

Many of the English words used today are taken from Greek or Latin words. Studying the roots of words can help students understand the meaning of words better, as well as help them with spelling. A root word is a word that can be made into a new word by adding a prefix and/or a suffix. The word can stand alone and has a meaning.

After students have studied the meanings of prefixes and suffixes of words, you can create a quiz game. Create questions that ask for the meaning of the word and award points for correct answers. For example:

Question: From looking at the following words, what do you think the word *bene* means?: benefit, beneficiary, benevolence, and benefactor

a. to take

b. good will

c. time

Answer: b. good will

Question: From looking at the following words, what do you think the word *dic* means?: dictionary, diction, and dictator

a. to speak

b. to rule

c. to know

Answer: a. to speak

Online Root Word Puzzles/Quizzes

Funbrain, www.funbrain.com/roots

Skillswise, www.bbc.co.uk/skillwise/words/spelling/wordbuilding/rootwords/

Similes and Metaphors

A simile is a comparison of two unlike things in which the words *like* or *as* are used, such as "She eats like a bird." A metaphor is a comparison of two unlike things in which no words of comparison are used: She sat at the foot of the mountain.

Activity ideas for similes and metaphors are:

- Compare unlike things by creating a book of metaphors with illustrations.
- Research well-known similes and metaphors and explain their meaning.

Give a simile or a metaphor to the students and have them explain the simile or metaphor. For example, "A math teacher is like an egg timer." Students need to explain why math teachers are like egg timers. Some answers may include: "They like to be perfect when done," "They like the fast pace of things," or "They like to turn things upside down and look at things from a different perspective."

The Dynamite Dictionary Game

"Improvement in vocabulary will result in improved writing skills only if the teacher is able to create a classroom that takes writing seriously" (Brynildssen, 2000). This means dedicating time to writing, spelling, and learning new words. The Dynamite Dictionary Game enhances vocabulary and takes little preparation, time, or materials. To play this game, students select a word from the dictionary that they think no one else will know. Then they write down the definition along with two other definitions that they make up. They read the definitions to the class, and the class tries to guess the correct definition. Each correct answer receives a point. I have the students keep track of their points each time we play the game.

ENHANCING ORAL COMMUNICATION SKILLS ■

Structure Conversation

One entertaining activity that improves communication skills is an activity called a Structure Conversation. The object of this activity is to improve communication and listening skills by building a structure with partners. The materials that are needed for this activity are a bag full of "junk" (paper clips, straws, cups, Popsicle sticks, buttons, spoons, and coins) and a barrier, such as a file folder. Two of every item is necessary. This activity is done with the partners sitting across from each other with the barrier between them so they can't see each other's workspace. Divide the materials between the partners so that each person has the same exact materials. The leaders build a structure or place their materials in a particular way on the table in front of them. Then the leaders must describe to their partners, in detail, using only words, what their structure looks like. Partners cannot look at what leaders have built and leaders can't look at how their partners are building their own structure. Leaders need to be very specific with their instructions to communicate their structure verbally, without using hand gestures. Words that they may need to use are *front, back, left, right, north, south, east, west, diagonal, parallel,* and *perpendicular.* Once a leader has communicated all of the directions on how to build his or her structure, the barrier is removed to see if the partner's structure looks identical. Hopefully, they do but if they don't, the two can communicate their misunderstandings. Then the roles are reversed. After doing this activity multiple times, students will improve upon giving and listening to directions. It's just amazing!

Mighty Monologues

A monologue is usually a long dramatic speech done by a single person. Having students develop their own monologue can help improve their communication and creativity skills. After watching and listening to monologue examples, students develop their own creative monologue. These monologue activities enrich, broaden, and improve their oral communication skills. Another benefit of this activity is that it takes very little time and no materials.

Topics for monologues can include:

- You are a ball in a tennis match. Describe what is going on.
- Your boss just fired you and you are rehearsing what to tell your mother.
- You are a dog that is placed in a kennel while your owners go on a weeklong vacation. Describe how you feel and what you are going to do.
- You are a: (Tell of your adventure or situation)

kitchen table	rock	bee
soccer ball	school bus	pencil
book in the library	diving board	mirror
half-eaten sandwich	fluffy pillow	cup
piece of paper	piece of grass	fly

Debates

Debates are an excellent way of involving multiple people in discussing a particular topic that they have researched or learned about and have a strong opinion. To organize a debate, select a topic for the class to research and discuss the pros and cons of the situation. I have found that relating topics of debates to students' real-life experiences will engage their motivation and curiosity.

Topic ideas for a debate can include:

- Should you be allowed to have an allowance without doing any chores around the house?
- Should the school impose school uniforms?
- Should you have to go to school six days a week?
- Should you have to have a set bedtime on a school night?
- Should the driving age be changed?
- Should you be able watch as much TV as you want to?

Drama

Drama is an exciting and novel area for students. My students just can't wait to act in a play or a skit. Their imaginations and creativity soar when they put on a theatrical production. Even with a small skit, students' enthusiasm overflows.

The benefits of drama experiences are numerous: problem-solving skills are utilized, motivation is increased, and creativity skills are enhanced. Putting on a big production with elaborate costumes and scenery is not necessary. Remember to start small with a play—costumes and props are the last details that should be addressed. The main objective is to enhance problem-solving and thinking skills, while also having fun with acting. Each drama experience will build up the students' level of expertise in acting and confidence. I have even done Shakespeare plays with my fourth graders, which they were excited to do.

Drama Resources Magazine

Plays: The Drama Magazine for Young People, by Sterling Partners, Inc. Their Web site is at www.playsmag.com

Foreign Language

Research has found that younger children can learn a foreign language easier than adults can (Brandt, 1997). Foreign language experiences offer students an excellent learning opportunity. Teachers can provide this experience by utilizing CD-ROMs and online courses or finding individuals to teach foreign language lessons. These individuals can be parents, other foreign language teachers, or even high school students studying a language. Creating an afterschool foreign language club where high school foreign language students teach other younger students benefits all involved. The high school students get practice in their language skills, while the younger students are taught a new language. There are various CD-ROMs that can help teach a foreign language. The following Web site introduces some basic language skills:

Word2Word: Free Online Language Courses, www.word2word.com/course.html

Socratic Seminars

A Socratic seminar is an activity that can be done in a small group or as a whole class. A topic is discussed and ideas are shared, leading learners to really understand the material through questions and discussions. A Socratic seminar can be used to discuss literature, current events, plays, classroom problems, or other situations. Before holding a seminar, students need to be knowledgeable about the topic and know the rules for holding a seminar. The teacher's role in the seminar is to be a facilitator and pose open-ended questions, such as, "Why do you think . . . ?" Teachers should not give their opinion; they should just keep the discussion going.

The rules for a Socratic seminar are:

Students sit in a circle.

Students take turns speaking.

Students don't need to raise their hand when they speak, but one student should not dominate the discussion. Everyone needs to be able to contribute.

Students need to support what they say, using evidence from what they have read or from personal experience.

If students disagree with what someone else has said, they should state what they disagree with and support their viewpoint, based on evidence. This should be done in a nonaggressive way.

Students really enjoy discussing a topic that interests them. After engaging in several Socratic seminars, students can lead the seminar themselves, and you are there simply to pose the discussion question in the beginning of each session. I have done a Socratic seminar with my fourth graders about the play *Romeo and Juliet*. Even though they didn't understand all the Shakespearean nuances, the students acted in a professional manner by adhering to the rules of the Socratic seminar and enjoyed having a discussion without much teacher direction.

Pantomime Activity

The use of body language is a way of communicating. After learning new material or reading a new book, have students create a miming skit that reflects what they learned or describes a character. It's a very challenging task for students to communicate without using words; it helps develop their problem-solving skills as well.

Miscellaneous Ideas for Developing Oral Communication Skills

Tell a Story. Storytelling is an oral tradition of passing stories from generation to generation for entertainment. A unit on storytelling is a good way for students to utilize and improve their communication skills.

Publish a Piece of Writing. Various publishers and Web sites give students a chance to get their own writing published. Following are some places to have students' works published:

Stone Soup
Submissions Department
P.O. Box 83
Santa Cruz, CA 95063
www.stonesoup.com

Skipping Stones
P.O. Box 3939
Eugene, OR 97403–0939
www.skippingstones.org/submissions.htm

Games. Everyone likes to play games. Many games, including Pictionary, Charades, and Twenty Questions, help students practice their communication skills. These are games that students will enjoy while they interact with others.

Listening Activities. Listening is very important in everyday life in order to be successful. Listening games such as Simon Says and Repeat After Me offer practice in listening skills.

Poems, Jokes, and Riddles. The last five minutes of class can be devoted to sharing poems, jokes, or riddles that students have created.

Investigate the Writing Style of Various Authors and Genres. Select a variety of authors and genres to read to the class. You can give a book talk about a particular book to pique students' interest or introduce a new author or genre.

Create a Newspaper for Important Issues. Students design a school newspaper about the happenings around the school and the community. You can discuss the importance of the jobs of reporters, printers, and editorial staff.

3

Creative Thinking

Everyone is creative, but some people excel more than others in creative thinking. So, what really is creativity? Creativity is the ability to imagine or invent something new by combining, improving, or changing an idea. Creative skills can be enhanced with practice—Nancy Andreasen (2005), a psychiatrist and neuroscientist, states that in order to improve creativity one needs to involve oneself in creative activities or situations.

Creative people can look at an idea or situation and find a way to improve it. They believe that a problem can be solved in various ways, not just one (Harris, 1998). Creative people are always seeking answers to problems or situations and want to know why things are the way they are. They are very curious people who love a challenge and suspend judgment until later. "Creative people see problems as interesting challenges worth tackling" (Harris, 1998).

The creative thinker needs to have perseverance, be flexible, and accept that mistakes are part of the creative process. Very famous creative people have made mistakes that have led to great success, including Charles Goodyear, inventor of the vulcanization process (tires); Spencer Silver, who invented Post-it Notes; and Alexander Fleming, discoverer of penicillin.

According to Harris (1998) and Winebrenner (2001), some characteristics of creative thinkers include the following:

- Displaying original ideas
- Being fluent in generating a variety of ideas
- Being able to elaborate on ideas
- Being very curious
- Recognizing relationships among unrelated objects
- Enjoying challenges
- Being optimistic
- Being able to suspend judgment

- Liking to use their imagination; fantasizing, daydreaming
- Seeing problems as interesting and as opportunities, and seeking them out
- Challenging assumptions
- Not giving up easily; persevering, working hard

Once you have identified students with strong creativity skills, teaching them the four components of creativity and having students practice them will help foster their creativity. Paul Torrance (1979), a pioneering researcher who studied creative thinking, describes the four components of creativity as fluency, flexibility, elaboration, and originality, categories that are still used today. Fluency pertains to generating as many ideas as possible to open-ended questions. Flexibility is looking at ideas in different ways or from different perspectives, whereas elaboration is embellishing or adding to an idea. Originality is having unique ideas and developing them. It is important to incorporate all of these components in order to establish and strengthen creativity within the classroom, especially to ensure that creative thinkers develop their gift. Naturally creative people may not even be aware that there are several ways to be creative—Jane is one example.

Jane

Jane was a student who enjoyed coming to class to learn something new every day. She could produce many ideas when brainstorming but never added any details to her finished projects. After teaching and practicing the four components of creativity (fluency, flexibility, elaboration, and originality) to the class, I noticed that Jane began to elaborate on her projects by adding those extra details. Engaging the class in creativity situations helped her make use of and hone her creative skills.

The following analysis activities are designed to assess students' creativity. Remember to use the results as a guide; other observations in the classroom are necessary to distinguish students' creative strengths. The ability to think creatively will help students in the future when they are faced with situations that need an original idea or something that needs to be fixed in some way. Creative individuals will be able to generate a wide variety of ideas to solve the problem.

■ ANALYSIS ACTIVITIES

Activity 1: Create a Product

Teacher Notes/Grading: Supply students with materials such as egg cartons, paper towel rolls, and boxes. Students should use these materials to create a useful product. Students should be able—orally or in writing, depending on their age—to describe their product in detail. There is no time limit for this activity, but most students will probably complete their product within thirty minutes. Some students may need more time because of their advanced and complex ideas.

Students can approach this activity in a variety of ways and there is no one correct answer to this activity. Check for the creativity components of originality, flexibility, and elaboration.

Directions:

Using "junk" (paper towel rolls, boxes, etc.), create a useful item for:
   Mom or Dad
   A person with a physical disability

Be prepared to explain how this new product works.

Activity 2: A Creative Box

Teacher Notes/Grading: Copy the activity for the student (see Directions, below), and make sure you have markers, crayons, or colored pencils available.

Students who excel in creativity will expand on their drawings of an original mystery box. They will probably create an odd-shaped box, not just a square or a rectangle. The embellishments that they add to the box will be detailed and unique, not just a bow on top. Creative students will also use a variety of colors to decorate their box. They may choose inanimate or intangible objects, such as love, to be in their box. Look for out-of-the-ordinary responses about items that can be included. Ordinary answers would be a pencil, a shirt, or a video. See the extraordinary mystery box example in Figure 3.1 as a sample.

Figure 3.1

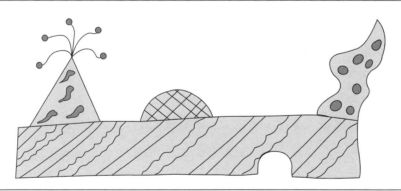

Directions:

Draw a wonderful, marvelous imaginary box. Add as many details as you can. Make it colorful and interesting. The box may be any size or shape you wish. Give your box a name and make the title as creative as possible.

Name of Box _____

What are all the things that could be in your wonderful box? Brainstorm a good descriptive list.

What can your marvelous box do? Are there items inside the box that can do special things? What could you do with this box?

Activity 3: What If . . . ?

Teacher Notes/Grading: Depending on grade level, students may respond by writing or drawing their answers.

Look for original and elaborate ideas. The out-of-the-ordinary answer demonstrates more creative thought. For example, if asked "What if cars had no wheels," saying "The car would not move" is not very creative. A creative response could be that the car would be a very expensive place to sit and look out at the stars.

Directions:

Read each "What if" statement and then respond to it.

a. What if cars had no wheels?

b. What if school was six days a week?

c. What if houses could fly?

Now create one of your own "What if . . ." statements for you or others to answer.

Activity 4: How Are These Alike?

Teacher Notes/Grading: Various age levels can do this activity. You may need to be the scribe for younger children.

Check for the fluency, flexibility, and originality of ideas.

Directions:

How are a clock and a calendar alike? How are they different? Illustrate your responses in a Venn diagram.

■ ENHANCING CREATIVE-THINKING SKILLS

Everyone is creative in his or her own way, but delving into and practicing the components of creativity will help students view and solve problems from different perspectives. Improving upon creativity will also help students elaborate and add detail to their projects.

Creative thinking leads people to unique outcomes or results. According to Alessandro Antonietti (1997), a professor at Catholic University in Milan, Italy,

> Children should learn that, when trying to think creatively, they may have to deal with many confusing, conflicting, and ambiguous ideas, so a quick and precise response cannot be expected.

Students need to learn to accept a period of uncertainty or anxiety, knowing that such troubles are necessary to develop creative approaches. (p. 75)

I believe that providing opportunities for students to use their creative-thinking skills in various scenarios where there is no right or wrong answer will help build upon their creative skills. When students use their creativity, they will realize that there are many possible answers.

Following are some units of study and activities to help enhance creative thinking.

Brainstorming

Brainstorming is an activity that leads students to think creatively on a given topic. The rules that I like to use for brainstorming are:

Quantity counts! The more responses, the better chance for great ideas.

Don't judge! All ideas are acceptable as long as you stay on the topic. There are no right or wrong answers.

Don't hesitate to be wild and crazy with ideas!

Combine, build, and spin off other ideas.

Don't stop too soon! Keep stretching for more ideas.

Stay on the topic! No unnecessary conversation allowed.

Effective brainstorming improves fluency and flexibility of ideas. I approach brainstorming with students in multiple ways. Sometimes we brainstorm as a whole class while other times individuals record their ideas on paper. I have the students create a booklet where they can record the date and the topic of each brainstorming session so they can see their improvement over time. At the end of the brainstorming session, students count up the number of responses (fluency) and select two or three ideas that they think no one else will have (originality). They then share their responses with the rest of the class. Students receive a point per response if no one else has an identical idea. For example, if one student's response is "brown crunchy leaves" and another's is "brown leaves," their ideas are different enough that they both would receive a point. I also have the students keep a running fluency graph (number of responses) on their brainstorming progress throughout the year.

To incorporate the flexibility component into brainstorming, students categorize their ideas. For example, ideas for "name things that are part of the fall season" may be leaves, wind, soccer, color changes, teachers, football, cold, and friends. Then these ideas are placed into categories such as: Weather (wind, cold), Sports (football and soccer), Things That Deal With Trees (leaves and color changes), and School (teachers and friends).

To really pique student interest, create a can called Brainstorming in a Can, and fill it with brainstorming topics. Students randomly select a topic from the can and start a brainstorming session. The great thing about brainstorming is that it doesn't take much time to do (five to ten minutes) and the rewards are wonderful.

Here are some brainstorming topics to help you get started.

List uses for:

Paper cup	Shoelaces	Old magazine
Napkin	Dryer lint	Pillowcase
Pen	Grass clippings	Newspaper
Paper clip	Milk carton	Soda straw
Rock	Spoon	Shoebox

Name things that:

Fly	Come in pairs	Are circular
Need each other	Are red	Are white and edible
Shrink	A fish might see	Glow

Name types of:

Animals that begin with the letter T (or any letter)	Rings
Rocks	Cheeses
Desserts	Breakfast foods

List words that have three, four, or five syllables

Name compound words that you find in school

Alphabet Brainstorm: Select a topic and brainstorm ideas that correlate with each letter of the alphabet.

SCAMPER

Young children love to use their imagination during play. SCAMPER is a technique created by Bob Eberle to improve imagination skills in children. SCAMPER is an acronym for:

S	Substitute	To take the place of another
C	Combine	To bring together or unite
A	Adapt	To adjust the purpose of something
M	Modify	To alter or change the form
	Magnify	To enlarge or make bigger
	Minify	To maker smaller
P	Put to Other Uses	To be used for other purpose than originally intended
E	Eliminate	To remove or get rid of
R	Reverse	To turn something around
	Rearrange	To change the order or adjust

The SCAMPER techniques can be used when you want students to take an object and change it in various ways. This obviously improves their creativity, using problem-solving skills and ideas to improve upon a situation. For more practice in these techniques, give students a picture of an object and ask them to redraw the object using one or more of the SCAMPER techniques. For example, the object of a winter hat can be combined with a radio to create a new type of hat that can be worn during the cold winter so that while you shovel snow you can dance to the music and keep your head warm.

For a culminating project, have students design an object that uses as many SCAMPER techniques as possible, along with a written description to explain what they used. Bob Eberle also wrote various SCAMPER books that include imaginative games, such as *SCAMPER: Creative Games and Activities for Imagination Development* (1997a) and *SCAMPER On: Creative Games and Activities for Imagination Development* (1997b).

Some activities that can be done for each SCAMPER technique are:

Substitute. Name an object and describe what else it can be used for instead. For example, a pizza can be used as a Frisbee.

Combine. Combine a refrigerator and a washing machine. Draw and describe how this new machine would work.

Adjust/Adapt. List things that are like a pillow.

Magnify/Minify/Modify. List ordinary items and what they could become if they were magnified. For example, a toothpick could become a flagpole.

Put to Other Uses. Think of other uses for a table, such as using it for a sled.

Eliminate. List items you can simplify by eliminating a part. For example, take the handle away from an umbrella and attach it to your head with a headband so your hands are free.

Rearrange/Reverse. Draw a picture upside down and concentrate just on the lines that are being made.

ABC Alliteration Book

Alliteration is the repetition of the same sound within a statement: Fuzzy flamingos find ferns to be fabulous. The ABC Alliteration project has students select a topic that they are very knowledgeable about and think of a word that correlates with each letter of the alphabet based on their topic. Research skills are needed to find words that begin with difficult letters, such as X and Z. Then, working with a partner, students combine their topics into one alliteration statement for each letter of the alphabet. For example, combining the topics of animals and food leads to "Enormous elephants eat eggplant." Incorporate technology into this project—have students use Microsoft Publisher to type up their alliteration statements into a booklet. Microsoft Publisher also has a greeting card template that students can use to type up their combined statements, one on each page. Students then print off the book and illustrate their statements. For a finishing touch, I hole-punch the pages and tie them together with string. This project incorporates all four components of creativity, as well as cooperation skills and novelty.

Creative People Unit

Gifted students often like to read autobiographies about scholars, leaders, and creative people—after all, these students will likely become the leaders and creative people that will make a difference in the future. Maker and Nielson (1995) suggest that "to learn how to deal with their own talent and possible success, gifted students should study creative and productive individuals" (p. 5).

Studying creative people, such as Walt Disney and Eric Carle, is a nice way to demonstrate the characteristics of creative people. Through research, students should realize that these individuals were not always creative and successful—they had to work hard at their craft in order to perfect it. Showing these individuals' failures to students reinforces the idea that everyone makes mistakes—something a gifted child can easily forget. For a culminating activity, students can research other creative people or create a poster board or brochure on the qualities of a creative individual.

Inventions and Inventors

Everyone would like to invent something to make his or her life easier. A unit study on inventions and inventors can lead students into devising their own inventions. This topic lends itself nicely to the science and social studies curricula. Some of the concepts that can be addressed in this unit are the characteristics and abilities of the inventors, where an idea for an invention comes from, and how an invention influences and changes our lives.

For a culminating activity, students can use their creative skills to invent something that would improve or simplify their lives, such as an organizer box that holds pencils, crayons, and lunch money and attaches to their books. Have them create a model of their invention to show how it would work, but remember: the thought process of their idea is most important. To round out the unit, plan an Invention Fair Night and have students set up their inventions in the classroom or hallway for others to view. They should be able to explain their inventions and answer other students' questions.

To round out this unit on inventions, study Rube Goldberg and the creative and complicated inventions he used to perform simple operations. Rube Goldberg was a Pulitzer Prize–winning cartoonist and artist. He created his famous invention drawings to use difficult means to accomplish a simple task. Gears, boots, animals, plants, and other ordinary objects were incorporated into his inventions, each one with many working components.

I have students draw their own Goldberg-style inventions to accomplish a simple task through a multistep invention. The Rube Goldberg Web site (www.rube-goldberg.com) shows excellent example drawings of this style of invention. This Web site also describes the process or steps that each invention goes through.

Inventor Resources

Mistakes That Worked: 40 Familiar Inventions and How They Came to Be, by Charlotte Foltz Jones (1991)

Rube Goldberg: Inventions, by Maynard Frank Wolfe (2000)

Problems to Pose

In this activity, students use their creative-thinking skills to answer questions. There are no right or wrong answers—check for original ideas and their thought process within their detailed explanations. This activity looks at the creative thought process.

- Which is slower, an oven or a refrigerator? Why? Explain your answer.
- Which is louder, happiness or fear? Why? Explain your answer.
- Which is softer, a cloud or a pillow? Why? Explain your answer.
- Which is happier, a piece of grass or a window? Why? Explain your answer.

In True Jeopardy Style

This activity pushes students to think of a variety of unusual answers while increasing fluency, flexibility, and originality of ideas. It sparks students' creativity because they are working backward to solve a problem and many answers are acceptable. In this activity, the answer is given and the students need to figure out what the question is.

Answer	Question Possibilities
6	What is 3 + 3? What is 2 × 3? What is half a dozen?
on the table	Where are my glasses? Where are the important math papers?
blue	What color are my eyes? What color is the sky?

Make up your own In True Jeopardy Style problems or have the students create their own to quiz each other.

Creative Designing

In the following activities, check students' originality and elaboration skills in each of their designs. Look for examples that incorporate new and original ideas into their final piece of work. For example, designing a toy that already exists without any alterations is not very creative. But if they take this toy and modify it to create a new function, they show creative thought. Students can elaborate on their examples by adding color, special features, and instructions for use.

- Design an original toy, animal, or object.
- Design a classroom of the future.
- Combine two things to create a new thing. Draw and write about your new thing. Examples can be animals, transportation vehicles, or school supplies. For example, a new animal might be an "eleguin" (half elephant and half penguin).

Detailed Improvement Activity

In this activity, students select an ordinary object and design improvements. They can design their new object by drawing or writing about it. Ideas for objects to improve upon can include: pen, bag, ruler, sponge, ice cube, notebook, soap, and towel. This activity practices the elaboration and originality components of creativity.

Line Design

These activities incorporate all four components of creativity.

Draw shapes or lines on a piece of paper. Have students make these shapes into a picture by adding as much detail as they can. Students should write a description of their drawing along with a title. See the example shown in Figure 3.2.

Using circles, students create as many things out of circles that they can think of. Students should add color and details to their drawings. The more creative responses include out-of-the-ordinary responses—drawings of a sun or a baseball are not very creative. Also, drawings that go outside the circle show more creativity.

Figure 3.2   Line Design Drawing

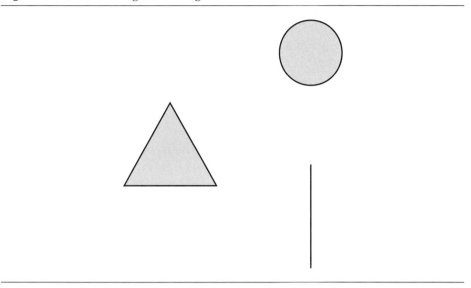

Character Elaboration

After reading a story, students select a character from the story and embellish on the character's personality or appearance. Using the elaboration and originality components of creativity, students brainstorm new attributes for this character. They should illustrate and write about their new-and-improved character.

Circle Story Starter

Students sit in a circle while the teacher tells the beginning of a story to the whole group. Then each student adds a sentence or two to the story, making sure the story flows nicely. This is done spontaneously. This activity enhances creativity, listening, and communication skills.

Some sample beginning story starters are:

- In the deep dark forest, there lived a . . .
- Two friends were walking along Main Street when . . .
- Maya looked up in the sky and saw . . .

Imagination Galore

Albert Einstein declared, "Imagination is more important than knowledge." Imagination plays a big part in children's lives; children who use their imagination enhance their creativity. Gardner (1991) claims that a child is given "enormous new power" and "allows the creation of works" when he or she uses imagination (p. 71). I believe that using one's imagination allows one to realize that things can be viewed from different perspectives and that new ideas stem from there. Older students can write on the following prompts; have your younger students describe their answers out loud or in a drawing. Activity ideas that use imagination are:

- Pretend that you have eyes in the back of your head. How would things be different for you?
- If you could be anywhere in the world right now, where would you be and why?
- Imagine that you won the lottery. What would you do first? Second? Third? How would your life change?
- Imagine what the future might look like in fifty years.

4

Critical Thinking

Critical thinking means having the skills to solve problems logically. Robert H. Ennis, accomplished author and emeritus professor at the University of Illinois, states that critical thinking involves both dispositions and abilities (Costa, 1991). According to Ennis, people who are creative thinkers "seek a clear statement of the thesis or question, seek reasons, look for alternatives, and [are] open-minded" (Costa, p. 12). They analyze arguments, make observations and inferences, and identify judgments.

All students need to be taught to think critically and logically about a situation or problem. Robert Howe's (Howe & Warren, 1989) research states that critical thinking includes three types of skills:

Enabling skills: observing, categorizing, comparing, and patterning

Processing skills: analyzing questions, inferring, making predictions, and identifying points of view

Operating skills: logical reasoning, creative thinking, and problem solving

Being able to think critically in a variety of ways helps gifted students in their everyday life as well as in their future learning experiences. Thinking skills, such as recognizing patterns, organizing information, making predictions, and developing problem-solving skills, should be nurtured and fostered in gifted children, even in the primary grades. I like to create a classroom atmosphere that gives students opportunities to wonder and reflect about a problem as well as allows them enough think time. This was especially helpful for Sam, a student I had a few years back.

Sam

Sam was a fifth grader who was always full of energy. He had problems sitting still during teacher-directed lessons. I introduced a problem involving Eskimos and how they captured seals without being heard on the ice. The class discussed the important clues to solve the puzzle. Many students were thinking creatively but critical thinking was necessary for this puzzle. Sam sat back, listened to the puzzle again, and then within a couple of minutes came up with the correct answer and the reasoning behind it. Sam needed opportunities where he could analyze information, problem solve, allow think time, and use his critical-thinking skills.

The following activities are designed to assess how well students recognize patterns, make comparisons, and show insight.

■ ANALYSIS ACTIVITIES

Activity 1: What Doesn't Belong?

Teacher Notes/Grading: This activity has students use their critical-thinking skills to determine which item in the group doesn't belong and explain why. They will need to compare and contrast the words. The students should be able to complete six out of the eight activities successfully. Note that some questions may have multiple answers; look for accurate explanations, even if they don't match the answer key.

Directions:

Read the group of words. Circle the word that doesn't belong and explain why.

1. cat   dog   bird   Why: _____

2. cow   pig   zebra   Why: _____

3. pie   cake   pretzel   Why: _____

4. paper   pencil   pen   Why: _____

5. spoon   plate   fork   Why: _____

6. dollar   nickel   penny   Why: _____

7. apple   orange   cookie   Why: _____

8. May   Tuesday September   Why: _____

Activity 1 Answer Key

1. cat   dog   (bird)   Why: It doesn't have four legs

2. cow   pig   (zebra)   Why: It doesn't live on a farm

3. pie   cake   (pretzel)   Why: It is not a dessert

4. (paper)   pencil   pen   Why: It is not a writing implement

5. spoon   (plate)   fork   Why: It is not a eating utensil

6. (dollar)   nickel   penny   Why: It is not a coin

7. apple   orange   (cookie)   Why: It is not a fruit

8. May   (Tuesday)   September   Why: It is not a month

Activity 2: Attribute Recognition

Teacher Notes/Grading: Learning to recognize patterns is a vital part of thinking critically. Students should be able to do this activity within ten minutes or so. These problems are more for primary students, but they can be modified for older students.

Students should be able to complete at least three out of the five problems correctly.

Directions:

Discover the rule for each problem.

All of these are pits:
20 30 40 50
None of these are pits:
25 17 35 67
What is the rule?

All of these are tads:
eyes mouth ears nose
None of these are tads:
leg arm toe knee
What is the rule?

All of these are pingos:
5 25 10 35 60
None of these are pingos:
27 89 34 11 78
What is the rule?

All of these are flishes:
mom dad wow pop
None of these are flishes:
dog cat car ton
What is the rule?

All of these are quilds:
pal pot pets bat
None of these are quilds:
pun sun pen nod
What is the rule?

Activity 2 Answer Key

Discover the rule for each problem.
All of these are pits:
20 30 40 50
None of these are pits:
25 17 35 67
What is the rule? All pits are multiples of 10.

All of these are tads:
eyes mouth ears nose
None of these are tads:
leg arm toe knee
What is the rule? All tads are parts of the body that are found on your head.

All of these are pingos:
5 25 10 35 60
None of these are pingos:
27 89 34 11 78
What is the rule? All pingos are multiples of 5.

All of these are flishes:
mom dad wow pop
None of these are flishes:
dog cat car ton
What is the rule? All flishes are palindromes.

All of these are quilds:
pal pot pets bat
None of these are quilds:
pun sun pen nod
What is the rule? If you spell the word backward, it makes a new word.

■ ENHANCING CRITICAL-THINKING SKILLS

"Thinking is essential to learning—any kind of learning. To learn requires an engagement and transformation of the mind" (Costa, 1991, p. 143). Teachers need to weave thinking skills across all disciplines in the curriculum so that thinking skills are reinforced. This is not always an easy task, but the rewards are wonderful: according to Cotton (1991), instruction in thinking skills promotes intellectual growth and fosters academic achievement gains.

Some characteristics that are common among gifted individuals with critical-thinking strengths are:

- Considering alternative solutions to problems
- Recognizing relationships and patterns
- Preferring complex and challenging tasks
- Being a keen observer; not missing anything

- Displaying original thinking
- Using higher-order thinking skills; liking abstract thinking
- Having a great deal of curiosity; being inquisitive
- Being intense when truly involved in an activity

Following are some activities to help enhance critical-thinking skills.

Six Thinking Hats

In the early 1980s, Edward de Bono created a technique called the Six Thinking Hats that helps students think about a situation from various perspectives, such as by looking for the good points or for the feelings behind the situation. Each colored hat represents a different type of thinking:

The white hat represents information or the facts

The black hat represents judgment or the bad points

The green hat represents creativity

The yellow hat represents the benefits or the good points

The red hat represents feelings, intuition, and emotions

The blue hat represents thinking about thinking

Showing students how to view situations from different perspectives by using different-colored thinking hats will help improve their thinking skills. Other benefits to using these thinking hat strategies are:

Ease of Use Within the Classroom. Teaching the meaning of each color hat takes only a small amount of time and can be reinforced throughout the day when different thinking is needed. A poster hanging on the classroom wall provides a great avenue for reinforcement.

Reduction of Conflict Within the Classroom. If a disagreement or conflict occurs between two students, the teacher can have them refer to the color of hat that each student should be wearing to see the other's thinking process as well as the appropriate hat needed to solve their issues together.

Increased Cooperation. When the whole class is a part of this community way of thinking, students can easily understand each other and learn in an environment where different ideas are accepted.

For a culminating activity for the Six Thinking Hats unit, I have students form groups of three and create a skit based on a situation that incorporates all six types of thinking. Each student selects two colored hats and brainstorms ideas on that type of thinking to incorporate into the skit. Each hat should be represented (speaking parts) in the skit at least twice. Students rehearse their skit to share with other classrooms or parents. I have used simple colored visor hats for props. Students switch their hats in the skit when demonstrating a different type of thinking.

Following are some of the skit situations that I have provided for my students. They randomly choose their skit out of a hat.

- Tim, Peter, and Natalie are thinking of ways to earn money to buy a new video game. Write a skit about them to show what they might do using the six thinking hats.
- What if you had to put money into your TV set to watch all programs?
- Someone gives you a large sum of money. Explain how you would decide to spend it.
- One evening you and a friend walk over to a neighbor's house to shoot baskets, but you find that your neighbor has to stay in and do homework. You and your friend think about what you could do instead.
- Mike, Diana, and Mary have invented a talking yo-yo. They are trying to persuade a manufacturer to produce the yo-yo.

Six Thinking Hat Resources

Six Thinking Hats for Schools: 3–5 Resource Book, by Edward de Bono (1991a)

Six Thinking Hats for Schools: 6–8 Resource Book, by Edward de Bono (1991b)

Creative Thinking: How to Use de Bono's "Six Thinking Hats" to Improve Your Thinking Skills, www.buildingbrands.com/goodthinking/08_six_thinking_hats.shtml

Analogies

An analogy is a comparison between two things that are alike or different in some way. When solving analogies, one uses analytical skills to compare the two words to discover the correct relationship between them and looks for two other words that have the same relationship. These puzzles improve vocabulary, flexible thinking, and analytical thinking. Smith (1997) concludes that analogies "are a useful way of encouraging thoughtful discussion about relationships among meanings of words." There are a variety of types of analogies: synonyms and antonyms, whole to part, general to specific, group to member, and thing to characteristic.

The great thing about analogies is that they can be used with every grade level as well as integrated into all areas of the curriculum. I have used picture analogies with second graders to enhance their recognition and analysis of relationships. Another benefit is that students can work through these puzzles at their own pace, without much teacher instruction. Creating their own analogies makes students a part of their own learning and also allows them to use higher-level thinking skills.

A simple analogy example is: skinny is to thin as fat is to obese. Analogies can vary in difficulty levels from easy to challenging. Following are some analogies to try.

Directions:

Look carefully at the relationship between the first two words. Find the word that is related to the third word in the same way the first two words are related, and circle that word.

Example: glove is to hand as sock is to: slipper   (foot)   toe

1. big is to small as short is to   length   height   tall

2. flower is to petal as guitar is to   string   play   music

3. orange is to peel as tree is to   oak   bark   wood

4. water is to liquid as ice is to   snow   freezing   solid

5. sheet is to bed as sock is to   leg   clothing   foot

6. butter is to toast as ketchup is to   mustard   hot dog   relish

7. milk is to refrigerator as ice
   cream is to   freezer   flavors   frozen

Answers

1. big is to small as short is to   length   height   (tall)

2. flower is to petal as guitar is to   (string)   play   music

3. orange is to peel as tree is to   oak   (bark)   wood

4. water is to liquid as ice is to   snow   freezing   (solid)

5. sheet is to bed as sock is to   leg   clothing   (foot)

6. butter is to toast as ketchup is to   mustard   (hot dog)   relish

7. milk is to refrigerator as ice   (freezer)   flavors   frozen
   cream is to

Analogy Resources

Analogies for the 21st Century, by Bonnie Risby (2001)

QUIA Vocab/Work Knowledge, www.quia.com/cb/7146.html (Jeopardy Game)

Fact Monster: Analogy of the Day, www.factmonster.com/analogies

I also like to use creative analogy puzzles that ask students to compare how one thing is like the other and then give their reasoning. This way, students use both creative and critical-thinking skills. They can also draw a picture that demonstrates their analogy to add more thought and detail to their answer. These types of creative analogies can be used in various subject areas. If you are studying electricity in science, you could create an analogy such as "A lightbulb is like _____ because _____." This will engage the student who is very creative but who may not be so good at science. These types of analogies are very easy to create and students will thoroughly enjoy solving them.

Active Analogies

Complete the statements. Be prepared to share your responses.

A piece of paper is like a _____ because

_____.

A computer is like _____ because

_____.

A rainbow is like _____ because

_____.

Create your own analogy statements along with reasons for the comparisons.

Logic Puzzles

Logic puzzles are great activities for all levels of students to strengthen their inferential skills, analyzing skills, and logical reasoning skills. These puzzles help students to think and work in an orderly manner and to read carefully for detailed information. When I introduced logic puzzles to my second graders, they just couldn't get enough of them. The benefits of logic puzzles are that students can work at their own pace without teacher instruction and there are a variety of difficulty levels.

Try the following puzzle. Use the grid to help solve the problem. If you figure out something is a no, place an N in the box. If you figure out something is a yes, place a Y in the box.

Favorite Food Logic Puzzle

The favorite fruits of Ben, Dave, Megan, and Heather are apples, grapes, pears, and bananas. Read the clues below to find each person's favorite fruit. Use the grid in Figure 4.1 to help you solve this puzzle.

1. Grapes are the favorite fruit of one of the girls.

2. Ben needs to peel his favorite fruit in order to eat it.

3. Megan and the boy who likes apples are in the same class.

4. Megan's favorite fruit comes in a bunch.

Figure 4.1   Logic Puzzle Grid

	Apple	Grapes	Pear	Banana
Ben				
Dave				
Megan				
Heather				

Answer to Fruit Logic Puzzle

	Apple	Grapes	Pear	Banana
Ben	N	N	N	Y
Dave	Y	N	N	N
Megan	N	Y	N	N
Heather	N	N	Y	N

After they have completed numerous logic puzzles and understand the important characteristics, I have my students create their own logic puzzles for others to solve. First, the students select a topic that they are interested in and create a completed grid with information such as peoples' names, the cars that they drive, and the color of those cars. Creating the clues for the logic puzzles is the next challenging step for students. They need to make sure that they don't give information away too easily and also that the puzzle can be solved with the clues given. After the students complete their grid and clues, I have them solve their own problem to make sure that it works. Students integrate computer technology into this project by using a word-processing program to type up the clues and use the table tool to create their grid.

There are various logic puzzle books with many levels of difficulty. Following are some logic puzzle resources:

Logic Safari: Book 1, by Bonnie Risby (2005)

Logic Puzzles to Bend Your Brain, by Kurt Smith (2003)

Primarily Logic, by Judy Leimbach (2005)

Logic Problems (play online), www.puzzles.com/projects/logic problems.html

Cryptology

Cryptology is the art and science of making (cryptography) and breaking (cryptanalysis) codes. Cryptography is the part of cryptology that deals with making codes or cipher systems so that others cannot read what is in the secret message. Cryptanalysis is the part of cryptology that deals with studying a secret message or a group of secret messages and breaking the system so you can read what it says without first knowing the key. *Cryptology* comes from the Greek words *kryptos* and *logos,* meaning "hidden word." This unit of study touches upon multiple subject areas, including math, science, social studies, and language arts. It also strengthens numerous skills, such as identifying patterns, problem-solving skills, and solving algebraic concepts. Creating invisible inks and applying this knowledge are skills used in the field of science; research the history of cryptology and write about codes to bring in the language arts component; in social studies, students can research when and how cryptography was used during wartime and other important periods, why secret codes were so crucial, and governmental issues about the use of cryptology.

Students thoroughly enjoy this unit of study because it involves deciphering and enciphering secret messages. What child doesn't like secret codes and mysterious messages? Solving different types of codes will pique students' interest, as well as have them use critical-thinking and problem-solving skills.

Cryptology vocabulary words to know are:

Plain Text: the message that is to be put into secret form

Cipher: the method of changing the plain text

Cipher Text: the secret version of the plain text

Key: explicit description of the cipher

Encipher: to change from plain text to cipher text

Decipher: to change from cipher text to plain text

Some types of cryptology codes include the following:

Lumping Words

Take out the spaces between the words and lump the words together. Use uppercase letters to make the codes harder to decipher.

| ILIKETORUN. | Answer: I like to run. |

Character Blocks

Put the letters of the words together in groups of two or more. Use uppercase letters to make the codes harder to decipher.

| SA MM AD EA CA KE. | Answer: Sam made a cake. |

Backward English

Write each word in the sentence or phrase backward.

| EHT OIDAR SI DUOL. | Answer: The radio is loud. |

Mirror Image Code

Create a message that is backward and can be read only using a mirror.

Pinprick Code

Using a piece of writing such as a newspaper, place pinpricks under letters to form your message. These marks are barely visible, but when the paper is held up to the light the secret message can be decoded.

Pig Pen Code

This code uses a tic-tac-toe matrix box; each letter of the alphabet and each symbol is created by referencing a letter position with the lines. A star or dot is placed in the position of the letter that you want.

A B C	D E F	G H I
J K L	M N O	P Q R
S T U	V W X	Y Z

The letter *p* would look like this in secret code.

```
 *
```

To make the ciphers harder, mix up the letters or create a different type of matrix box, such as one with crisscross or diagonal lines.

Cipher Clock Codes

This code uses two circular wheels divided into twenty-six parts, one smaller than the other, that are secured with a paper fastener. Each letter of the alphabet is placed in a section of the wheel. To decode a message, locate the coded letter on the outside circle. Line up the inner wheel with the letter on the outside wheel.

Have your students decode the following secret messages using the cipher clocks shown in Figure 4.2.

Figure 4.2   Cipher Clock

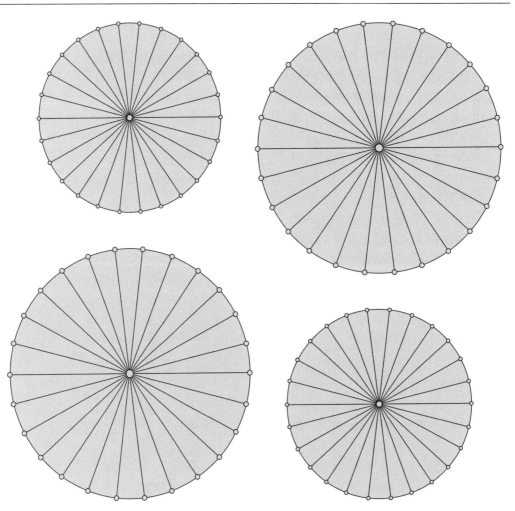

Cipher Clock Secret Messages

Using the cipher clock, decode the following secret messages. Remember to use decoding strategies, such as trying to figure out a two- or three-letter word first. Good luck!

1. WPKT P CXRT SPN.

2. EXMMV XKKFSBOPXOV

3. EZOLJ HP LCP OPNTASPCTYR

4. VEBBEM JXU RQDA EV JXU HYLUH.

5. IXGIQ ZNOY IUJK.

6. JXYDA SHUQJYLUBO.

Answers to the Cipher Clock Secret Messages:

1. Have a nice day.

2. Happy Anniversary

3. Today we are decoding messages.

4. Follow the bank of the river.

5. Crack this code.

6. Think creatively.

Mastermind

The strategy game of Mastermind is also based on secret codes. Playing this game improves each student's reasoning and problem-solving skills while having fun. My students enjoy playing this challenging game with a partner during their free time. They use their inference, analytical, and logical skills to decipher the secret code. I have the students use the Mastermind board game as well as an interactive Mastermind Web site (http://thinks.com/java/mastermind/mastermind.htm). If you don't have this game, you can just have the students use paper and crayons or markers to play it.

Arithmetic Cryptology

Arithmetic cryptology codes can be simple or very challenging. This type of code uses letters to represent numbers in a math problem. Students use critical-thinking skills to solve these puzzles. The task is to figure out the number that each letter represents. Each letter represents a single-digit number from 0 to 9, a number cannot be used for a different letter within the same problem, and the left-hand digit cannot be zero.

Students need to remember that some columns may carry over into the next column. I have created the following cryptography puzzles to challenge student's critical-thinking skills. Some problems may have multiple answers.

If M = 3 and A = 6, then T = _____?

MA	F
+ AM	+ G
T T	9
(36 + 63 = 99)	This problem has multiple answers.

R A T

+ I N

S A P

(307 + 95 = 402)

ONE	FOUR
+ ONE	+ FIVE
TWO	NINE
(231 + 231 = 462)	(2970 + 2186 = 5156)

CAT	SUN
+ DOG	+ RAY
PET	HOT
(523 + 170 = 693)	(469 + 281 = 750)

SEED	ICE
+ SUN	+ CUBE
GROW	COLD
(8221 + 836 = 9057)	(174 + 7524 = 7698)

After studying this unit, may choose from multiple options for students a culminating project:

1. Create your own code for others to solve. Explain how your code works and provide examples of messages in code. Display your work on a poster board or in booklet form.

2. Create a cryptology calendar (month or year) of important events that happened in history. Find an important event that happened on each day and put that information in code for others to solve daily. Remember to include an answer key.

3. Solve various cryptology puzzles.

Note: These puzzles can be found in various critical-thinking math books. I usually make up my own cryptographic arithmetic puzzles as well as have students create and solve each other's puzzles.

Additional Cryptology Resources

The Usborne Book of Secret Codes, by Eileen O'Brien and Diana Riddell (1997)

Codemaster Book #1: How to Write and Decode Secret Messages, by Marvin Miller (1998)

MENSA Secret Codes for Kids, by Robert Allen (1997)

Mastermind, http://thinks.com/java/mastermind/mastermind.htm

Sudoku Puzzles

With sudoku—a Japanese number-placement puzzle—students utilize their problem-solving and logic skills to arrange the digits 1 through 9 in a 9-by-9 grid so that a number appears only once within each column, row, or region (3-by-3 grid). There are no calculations and no guessing. Everything is based on logic. With clues given, students use the process of elimination strategy or the "what if" strategy to help solve these puzzles. These puzzles come in various difficulty levels and to challenges even the best problem solvers.

Sudoku Puzzle Web Sites and Resources

Sudoku, from Parragon Publishing

Sudoku, www.sudoku.org.uk/

Said What?, www.saidwhat.co.uk/sudokus/index.php

Critical-Thinking Resources and Web Sites

Stories With Holes, by Nathan Levy (various dates)

Exidor's Logic Puzzle Place, www.thakur.demon.nl/

Games That Enhance Problem-Solving Skills

Chess

Checkers

Ice Blocks, by Gamewright, Inc.

5

Interpersonal and Intrapersonal Intelligence

Interpersonal and intrapersonal intelligences are placed together in this chapter because they are closely related: both revolve around the importance of people. Interpersonal giftedness deals with the ability to interact with and read people while intrapersonal intelligence deals with oneself. The interpersonal intelligence is looked at first in this chapter.

Interpersonal intelligence is the ability to perceive people's moods, feelings, and intentions and to respond appropriately to these signals. This intelligence also involves being able to read a person's gestures or facial expressions. People who are comfortable in front of crowds, show leadership qualities, like group sports and clubs, have several friends, and like to give advice to others exhibit strong interpersonal skills. Students who are strong in this area are usually easy to identify because they are the leaders in the classroom, the students whom others go to for help and who work well with others.

Some characteristics that are common among gifted individuals with interpersonal strengths are:

- Being concerned about right and wrong; having empathy for others
- Being intense when truly involved in an activity
- Enjoying socializing with others
- Being a natural leader
- Working well with others
- Giving advice to others who have problems

- Being sought out by others for their company
- Being self-confident and well organized
- Being highly verbal
- Being a keen observer; not missing anything

The most effective way to identify students with strong interpersonal intelligence is through observation. There is no real test that can assess interpersonal skills. Observing students during free time can give insight into their strengths. The checklist of interpersonal qualities shows the behaviors to look for. The checklists certainly helped me with Elizabeth.

Elizabeth

Elizabeth was a natural leader in the fifth-grade classroom and exhibited strong interpersonal skills. She was always aware of other people's feelings and concerned when others were unhappy. When she was in third grade, many students thought that she was just a bossy know-it-all. She had a forceful way of presenting herself or her ideas that many students didn't like. Throughout the three years that I had her, she really came into her own by using my activities to hone her leadership skills and empathy for others. Many students came to accept her and went to her for advice.

The following activities are designed to assess how students deal with others in various situations. Remember that there are no right answers to these problems; they show how one deals with others.

■ INTERPERSONAL ANALYSIS ACTIVITIES

Activity 1: Social Situation Number 1

Teacher Notes/Grading: Grading this activity is not easy or straightforward. Look for examples of the student's leadership qualities as well as empathy and compassion for others.

You are planning your big birthday party. Your mom tells you that you can invite only eight of your friends to the Party Zone. You have ten close friends that you want to invite to the party. What do you do? What decision do you make about inviting your friends? What do you tell your mother? Is Mom being fair? Are there any alternatives that you can think of doing so as not to hurt anyone's feelings?

Activity 2: Social Situation Number 2

Teacher Notes/Grading: Grading this activity is not easy or straightforward. Look for examples of students' leadership qualities as well as empathy and compassion for others. Students with strong interpersonal skills will try to solve the argument between the two students, like a mediator, and will also be the ones who will take charge and lead the group to completing the project.

Your teacher asks you and two of your classmates, Peter and Susie, to work on a social studies project together. Your group's assignment is to research an animal and create a project that describes where it lives, what it eats, and what it looks like. Where do you start? How do you determine who will do what?

Susie and Peter start disagreeing about how the project should look. What do you do? How do you stop or solve the argument between Peter and Susie?

ENHANCING INTERPERSONAL SKILLS ■

Students who are talented in the interpersonal intelligence excel in discussions, small group work, and social situations, and have a knack for organizing people. These students have a keen sense of others' feelings and emotions and have empathy for others.

Some activities that will benefit this style of learner are:

- Brainstorming
- Peer editing
- Group discussions
- Cooperative learning activities within the classroom
- Peer tutoring
- Group games
- Group research projects
- Drama experiences—plays, skits, and debates
- Writing to a pen pal from a different culture or part of the world
- Creating a club for others to join based on books, hobbies, or areas of interest

Interviews

Conducting interviews of community leaders, teachers, or others helps students gain experience with questioning skills, social skills, and empathy. For practice, students may select an individual with whom they are familiar to devise their first interview. Topics can include how life was in their grandparents' time or how the cafeteria staff selects what to serve and why. Students should devise their questions for the interview beforehand and be prepared to take notes. This activity is also good for improving note-taking and listening skills.

Share What You Learn

Any time the students learn a new skill, have them teach the steps involved to others. The new activity can include a dance, musical instrument, computer software program, or craft. This activity lets students who excel in interpersonal skills be leaders, share their passion with others, and feel comfortable in their strength area. Accordingly, renowned author Joan Franklin Smutny (Smutny, Walker, & Meckstroth, 1997) talks about sharing students' work as a "discovery process, that everyone has a role to play in this process, and that each of them has a unique contribution to make to the world around them" (p. 74).

Role-Play Characters

After reading a book, students role-play a character of their choice to gain a better understanding of the character. Students should share the character's main traits, purpose, and experiences through their role-playing. They should rehearse their skit, dress up in character, and use props if necessary, to share with others.

Create a Game

Working in small groups, students develop a game the class can play. They should create a poster with the rules and the purpose of the game on it. Students will need to explain their game and be able to answer questions for clarification of the rules of the game. Students who work together to create a game develop cooperative learning skills. Examples of games can include creating easier methods for practicing spelling words, such as basketball spelling. The rules for this example are:

Divide the class in half.

Students who spell a word correctly can shoot a foam ball from a certain distance into the trash can.

If they make it in the basket, they receive points.

The next team continues the same process.

The game continues until a certain point level is scored or a time limit has passed.

Challenge: Make up a game with popcorn and containers. Other materials can be used.

Challenge: Make up a game using only erasers.

Turn to a Partner

In this activity, two students turn to each other and describe what they have just learned. They should state it in their own words. This activity should be used after new material has been taught and should take no more than five minutes. To put another spin on this activity, have one student just listen while the other talks, and then have the listener restate what the first student said. This is a great listening activity.

Advice Column

Students with strong interpersonal intelligence have a good sense of empathy for others (Armstrong, 1994). Other students usually seek out these students for advice, and one fun project for these students is designing an advice column for the school or classroom newsletter. To encourage the whole class to practice empathy, you could also do this activity much like a "Dear Abby" column: have each student write a question, and randomly throughout the year select a question and have every student write a reply. For example, a student may want advice on how to work out a problem with a friend. The whole class will write responses to this problem and the student who needed the advice will enjoy the variety of responses. The questions can be written anonymously; only the teacher will know who wrote the questions in order to give responses to the right students.

Moving Writing

In this writing activity, one student starts writing a story; the beginning of the story is passed on to another student, who adds to the story. This process continues until the story is done. The story is then shared with the class and discussed within small groups. Students can discuss how well the story flowed, the good points of the story, the need for improvements in the story, and how everyone cooperated to complete this task. Have the students choose the topic for teacher approval and discuss beforehand the appropriate rules and etiquette for the Moving Writing activity.

This activity can be used with all grade levels. If you are using this activity with primary age students, a verbal discussion may work better because of their limited writing skills.

Community Service Projects or Events

Real-life community service projects or events can be the focus for student research projects and can correlate with the social studies curriculum. Students select a community problem or event that they feel strongly about, and try to change or improve it. They can do anything from creating a recycling program within their school or community to coordinating a food drive for the Food Bank. This student-directed activity will help them connect their learning to real-world experiences.

———————————●●●———————————

Individuals who excel in intrapersonal intelligence are those who can get in touch with their own feelings, emotions, and weaknesses. Emotions play a very important role in setting priorities and goals. Students who are capable of getting in touch with their own feelings like to work independently toward a goal that they set for themselves. They also have high self-esteem, know their desires in life, and learn from their failures.

Some characteristics that are common among gifted individuals with intrapersonal strengths are:

- Having a great imagination; being a daydreamer
- Having interests that they don't want to share with others
- Having perfectionist tendencies; setting high goals for self

- Recognizing own strengths and weaknesses
- Having high self-esteem
- Being self-directed, independent
- Being intense when truly involved in an activity
- Learning from their failures and success

Assessing intrapersonal strengths in students is not easy or definitive. For teachers, gathering as much information as possible will be helpful in understanding the type of learner each of these students is. You will be able to plan better for these students because they tend to want to work by themselves, are able to set goals, understand their own strengths and weaknesses, and are independent and strong willed. It's helpful to plan opportunities for these students to work alone and to set goals for part of their learning, like I did for Sarah.

> ### Sarah
>
> Sarah's intrapersonal skills were very strong for a fifth grader. She knew that she was a very talented writer and artist but also knew that mathematics was one of her weaker areas. When presented with a challenge, she was thoroughly engaged in the activity and set high goals for herself in completing the task. Sarah usually chose to work alone on projects because she knew what she wanted to do and didn't want to have to deal with other people's viewpoints. Knowing her style of learning preference, I made a point of giving her opportunities to be able to work alone on some projects.

To find out what your students like to do, supply students with a list of activities and have them rank them in the order they would like to do them. The list of activities can be writing a story, playing a game with friends, solving math problems, doing puzzles, working alone on a project, and reading a book. This information shows a student's activity preference, which can be used for planning future learning experiences.

The following analysis activities are helpful for gathering information on students' self-knowledge. Remember, there are no right or wrong answers; the activities should be used to help you both get to know your students better and know how they feel about themselves. Through these analysis activities students may demonstrate their strengths and weaknesses, as well as give you a glimpse of how they view themselves as learners. The self-portrait activity is especially interesting to assess because you may see their unique qualities.

■ INTRAPERSONAL ANALYSIS ACTIVITIES

Activity 1: Self-Portrait

Teacher Notes/Grading: There are no right or wrong answers. This activity will demonstrate how students view themselves.

Directions:

Draw a self-portrait.

Activity 2: Special Space

Teacher Notes/Grading: There are no right or wrong answers. This activity demonstrates how the student would like to design his or her own special space. Their goals, strengths, and weaknesses may be shown in their drawing.

Directions:

Draw your own "special space," as you would like it to be.

Activity 3: I Am Like . . .

Teacher Notes/Grading: Remember that there are no right or wrong answers. Students should draw an animal and then explain why they are like that animal. The explanation of the animal is the most important part because it provides you with insight into how students feel about themselves. For example, a child might select a mouse and explain that he is small, quiet, and quick, and keeps to himself. It's important to know how students view themselves for future planning options. You can also pair up students who have selected the same animal for similar reasons to work together later.

Directions:

Draw an animal that fits each description. Write a sentence or two about your drawing.

Most of the time I am like a . . .
Sometimes I am like a . . .
On rare occasions I am like a . . .

ENHANCING INTRAPERSONAL SKILLS ■

Providing opportunities for these students to complete an independent study, allowing self-paced instruction, and providing options for units of study and homework are strategies that can be used for these types of learners. Since most of these students prefer to be by themselves, we as teachers need to give them time during the day to do this.

The following activities will help students with a strong intrapersonal intelligence.

Interest Survey and Comparison

An interest survey encourages students to look at their interests, goals, and dreams and to pursue these areas in much more detail through an independent study project. See the Interest Survey and Interest Comparison activities below.

Interest Survey

Complete the following questions about yourself.

What kinds of books do you like to read?

In your free time, what two activities do you like to do?

What are your hobbies?

What things do you collect? How long have you been collecting these items?

What is your favorite subject in school? What is your least favorite subject? Why?

What do you want to do when you grow up?

If you could invent something, what would it be? Explain.

If you could pursue any topic of interest for a school project, what would it be? Why?

Interest Comparison Activity

In this activity, answer the following comparison questions and explain your reason for the comparison.

1. What food is like you? Why?

2. What emotion is like you? Why?

3. What television program is like you? Why?

4. What season is like you? Why?

If I Could Be . . .

Have students select an individual they would like to be and ask them to explain why. In their writing piece, they should be specific about why they selected this individual, whether because of their inventions, products, or accomplishments. These individuals can come from history or even be characters in a book.

Another topic option is to have students select an animal or object that they would like to be and describe why. This activity causes students to look deep within themselves to reflect on their emotions and feelings and to make comparisons to individuals, objects, and animals. This topic can be helpful when dealing with younger students, and answering out loud is fine if they're too young to write.

My Autobiography

Students write an autobiography of their life so far. They should include their accomplishments, special events that have changed their life, and lessons that they have learned. As a sequel to this book, students can describe what the future will hold for them and write about how they see their future. This can include their goals, aspirations, and life expectations. Younger students can create collages out of magazine pictures or draw their autobiography.

T-Chart Diagram

Students create a T-Chart diagram that lists their strengths and weaknesses. A T-Chart diagram has two columns; students list their strengths on one side and their weaknesses on the other. This activity has students reflect on what they are good at and in what areas they can improve. Remember, these students like to set goals for themselves; this can also lead students to create a resolution to improve upon one or two of their weak areas, such as organization.

Me Box

Students create a special box that contains memories, awards, pictures, or any other personal items that they want to include about themselves. They should decorate the outside as well as the inside of the box to reflect their own style. The box can be shared with others if they want to, but it's fine if students create this special box just for themselves. This can be an ongoing project throughout the year.

One-Minute Thinking Period

After students have learned challenging new material, give them one to two minutes to reflect on what they learned and how they can connect it to their own life to make it more meaningful. Their thoughts don't need to be shared with the rest of the class. For example, after learning about fractions in mathematics, students may connect this concept to how they will split a large pizza with their six friends so that everyone gets an equal share. If they are learning about Mexico's holidays, they may relate the differences between the Mexican holiday of the Day of the Dead and our Halloween.

Miscellaneous Intrapersonal Ideas

Have Students Keep a Diary or Journal. Give students time during the day or week to jot down ideas, thoughts, or dreams in their diary. This will keep them in touch with their feelings, dreams, emotions, and goals.

Encourage Students to Set Goals for Themselves in Relation to School, Family, Hobbies, Interests, and the Community. Students can create a list of their goals, which can be kept so they can check off and add to it when they have time. This is also a nice way for them to reference what they need to do in order to achieve their goal.

Have Students Self-Pace Their Own Learning. The student and teacher need to meet to create a contract for the learning requirements, such as making sure that deadlines are being met and how long a project will take.

Have Students Keep a Portfolio of Work or Ideas. Students can keep a file where they can put projects for them to look at and work on. This file doesn't need to be shared with others.

Give Students Time to Meditate or Daydream. These students enjoy being by themselves to think, wonder, and work. Provide time to allow students to daydream or meditate about their lives, goals, and feelings. Creating a special area in the classroom for them to be by themselves will benefit these students.

Let Students Work Alone on Projects. Provide opportunities for students to work alone on projects so that they can be comfortable with their own learning.

6

Mathematics

Mathematically gifted students' needs are very different from those of their peers. The pace at which they learn, the depth of their understanding, and their interest level in mathematics should all be taken into account every time you teach the subject to the class (Johnson, 2000). Developing a program for mathematically gifted students should not focus on computation, but should delve into mathematical reasoning, problem solving, and discovery learning (Miller, 1990).

The ability to use numbers effectively and to reason well are characteristics of a person with strong logical and mathematical skills. Recognizing patterns, making inferences and calculations, and seeing relationships are just some of the skills that students with strong mathematical strengths should develop. Characteristics that are common among gifted individuals with mathematics strengths are:

- Recalling information quickly and accurately
- Trying to discover how things work
- Having a great deal of curiosity; being inquisitive
- Being intense when truly involved in an activity
- Using higher-order thinking skills; liking abstract thinking
- Recognizing relationships and patterns
- Preferring complex and challenging tasks
- Considering alternative solutions to problems
- Being interested in numerical analysis
- Reasoning effectively and efficiently

Students with strong mathematical skills like to compute numbers in their head, figure out logic puzzles, play strategy games, and put things into categories, and truly enjoy learning new math skills. I have had numerous students who were gifted in mathematics and I wanted to make sure I provided enough challenge for them. One such student was Tim.

Tim

Tim was a student who just thrived when I gave him math challenges. He wanted to spend the whole class time trying to figure out solutions to problems, and he could solve them quickly and easily. As a teacher, I wanted to make sure that I was meeting his needs while letting him thrive in his area of strength, so I kept searching for challenging tasks. I partnered Tim with another gifted math student because they shared common strengths. Both students pushed each other to solve problems and reach their own potential. I have always said that it is beneficial for students with similar abilities to be together, and it certainly worked for Tim.

■ ANALYSIS ACTIVITIES

The following analysis activities are designed to assess a variety of math-related concepts.

Activity 1: Mental Math

Teacher Notes/Grading: Slowly, read the following problems to the student. The student should mentally calculate the answer. Do as many as possible to test the student's limit; record the student's responses. This activity can be used for a variety of grade levels; a second grader may get all of these correct because she is really strong in calculating numbers, whereas a fifth grader may get only five correct. Students who get five out of the seven correct are strong in mental math.

    a. $7 + 5 - 8 = $ _____ (4)

    b. $4 + 2 - 3 + 5 + 5 - 9 = $ _____ (4)

    c. $6 + 2 - 4 + 6 + 7 + 12 = $ _____ (29)

    d. $42 + 6 + 8 - 9 + 3 + 12 = $ _____ (62)

    e. $23 + 6 - 13 - 7 - 4 + 17 + 15 + 2 = $ _____ (39)

    f. $16 + 5 - 13 \times 4 + 8 - 19 \times 2 + 23 - 39 + 2 = $ _____ (28)

    g. $12 + 9 \div 3 \times 9 + 122 - 68 - 6 + 61 \times 2 = $ _____ (344)

Activity 2: Place Value

Teacher Notes/Grading: This activity is designed to assess primary-age students' understanding of place value. Create 3×5 cards of the following numbers and have the students read out loud the number on each card. Ask them the following questions about what specific numbers represent. If they can get four or five correct, they have a strong understanding of place value.

Card A	17	What does the 7 represent?
Card B	654	What does the 6 represent? What does the 5 represent?
Card C	2,892	What does the 9 represent? What does the 8 represent?
Card D	5,639	What does the 5 represent? What does the 6 represent?
Card E	18,724	What does the 1 represent? What does the 8 represent?
Card F	587,632	What does the 5 represent? What does the 8 represent?

Activity 3: Creative Problem Solving

Teacher Notes/Grading: Students will read each question and record their answers. Not all of the questions need to be answered. You may want to select one or two or have students select the ones that they want to do. There are no right or wrong answers for these problems. This activity asks students to use their creativity, so look for unique and creative answers. For example, a creative answer for measuring the distance to the cafeteria maybe be solved by walking heel to toe all the way there. Then when you have a ruler, measure your foot and multiply that number by the number of "feet" it took to get to the cafeteria. A lunch box or an 8-1/2" × 11" sheet of paper may also be used to measure. Look for out-of-the-ordinary responses that may work.

   Directions: Read and solve each problem and record your answer.

   a. How would you weigh an elephant without placing it on a scale?
   b. How would you measure the distance from the cafeteria to your classroom without a ruler?
   c. How would you tell what time it is if you didn't have a watch or a clock?

Activity 4: Longest Number Card Game

Teacher Notes/Grading: Create sets of 3 × 5 cards for the following problems; each number and symbol should have its own card. Ask students to create a true equation using as many cards as possible. Students may use each card only once.

Set A	2 2 4 6 8 7 0 1 + + − × ÷ =
Set B	6 4 1 1 0 2 3 + + − × ÷ =
Set C	6 6 1 2 9 4 7 + + − × ÷ =
Set D	1 2 3 4 5 6 7 8 9 + + + + − − × × ÷ ÷ =

■ ENHANCING MATHEMATICAL SKILLS

Strong mathematical students need to be introduced to a variety of topics to enhance their learning. I have used many topics that are novel and are not usually covered within the regular mathematics curriculum. Gifted mathematical students need to be aware that math is not always just about numbers and that sometimes there is more than one answer to a problem.

Mathematically talented students exhibit multiple characteristics, such as:

- Learning and understanding mathematical ideas quickly
- Working systematically and accurately
- Thinking logically and seeing relationships
- Making connections between the concepts they have learned
- Identifying patterns easily
- Being able to explain their reasoning and justify their methods when solving a problem
- Taking a creative approach to solving problems
- Being persistent in finding a solution to a problem

Following are topics that I have used for math enrichment and acceleration activities. Many of these activities also can be used for improving critical- and creative-thinking skills.

Follow Alongs

Follow Alongs are mental math problems that I do with students to get them engaged, enhance their mental math capacity, and improve their listening skills. The rules for Follow Alongs are:

You need to solve the problem mentally. You are not allowed to write the problem down on paper.

You may not talk.

Listen very carefully because I will not repeat.

When I say "equals," if you know the answer go to the board and when I count to three, write your answer.

I don't grade students on this activity, so it's okay if they don't go to the board or if they get the answer wrong. Below are some examples of Follow Alongs that can be modified according to students' needs.

Follow Alongs

$4 + 6 + 12 - 8 = 14$
$12 + 15 - 7 + 4 + 8 = 32$
$25 - 8 + 7 + 6 \times 2 - 8 + 3 = 55$
$98 - 28 + 15 - 23 + 3 + 65 = 130$
$14 - 7 \times 2 + 35 - 26 - 9 - 9 \times 3 + 67 - 8 = 74$
$40 - 8 - 19 \times 2 + 17 + 7 \times 3 - 23 - 16 - 9 = 102$
$17 \times 2 - 9 + 48 - 17 - 6 - 25 - 4 - 7 + 2 = 16$
$64 \div 8 \times 6 + 24 \div 9 - 6 + 59 + 66 - 32 - 66 = 29$
$46 + 26 \div 8 \times 10 - 23 + 69 - 6 \div 2 + 39 = 104$
$29 \times 2 + 36 - 48 + 4 \div 2 \times 6 + 78 - 22 = 206$
$32 \div 4 \times 3 - 12 + 24 \div 9 \times 4 + 9 \div 5 \times 9 = 45$
$42 + 39 \div 9 \times 4 \div 6 + 28 - 2 \div 4 \times 2 + 5 \div 3 = 7$
$36 \times 3 - 59 - 6 + 26 \div 3 + 178 - 1 \div 2 + 65 = 165$
$18 + 56 - 2 \div 2 - 28 \times 7 + 38 - 14 \div 4 - 25 = -5$
$63 + 69 - 12 \div 10 \times 4 - 36 + 58 \div 2 + 57 = 92$

Study of Different Number Systems

The study of multiple number systems allows students to analyze the similarities and differences among them. This unit can also lead into the study of different base systems, such as base 2, which can aid students in understanding the base 10 system better.

To start this unit, I ask students the name of our number system—which most don't know. It's interesting that they have learned how to count and how to use our number system, but have never been formally introduced to its real name! Discuss the Arabic-Hindu number system's unique feature of being a place-value system and how it has changed throughout the years. Once students understand the difference between a place-value and a counting-number system, start delving into studying other number systems. Some of the number systems to touch upon are Roman, Egyptian, Babylonian, Greek, Braille, Chinese, Japanese, and Mayan.

The four components of creativity can be incorporated into the study of different number systems. To develop fluency, have students write as many Roman numerals as they know and what each number represents before studying about them. Group the different number systems into categories and find as many classifications of these number systems as you can to use the component of flexibility. To develop the elaboration component, have students predict how our number system will look in the future (it may help if they look at the details in the appearance of the Arabic-Hindu numerals and how they have changed throughout the years). Creating a unique number system incorporates the originality component of creativity.

After students have studied these number systems, I have them create their own. Use the rubric that lists the requirements for this project as a guide.

Teacher Notes: Here is a sample of the grading rubric I use for the number systems project. It can be adapted for almost any activity in the book.

As a follow-up activity, check students' understanding by using the Number System Check Up worksheet (Figure 6.1). This sheet can be modified in any way you like.

Number System Project Descriptor

PARTS	Possible Points	Student Points	Teacher Points	ATTRIBUTES
PHASE ONE Describing the Number System	4			Tell if the number system is a place-value or a counting system and the characteristics that make it this type
	2			Creative name for number system
	8			Follow the place-value or counting system rules
PHASE TWO Number Creation	12			Draw symbols 0 or 1 through 10, 100, and 1,000 and other important numbers
	4			Label each symbol with a number
	10			Neatly and creatively drawn
PHASE THREE How the Number System Works	8			Describe (in words) the history of the number system
	5			Describe (explain in detail) how it works and how to combine symbols to make numbers
	8			Show how to add, subtract, multiply, and divide numbers—designate two-digit problems for each
PHASE FOUR System Evaluation	8			Compare and contrast your system to the Arabic-Hindu number system using a Venn diagram
PHASE FIVE Overall Presentation	4			Present the project in an organized and unique way (booklet, poster, etc.)
	5			Complex ideas
	5			Neat and attractive appearance
	5			Accurate spelling and grammar
	9			Creativity
	3			Being prepared (Hand project in on time)
Total	**100**			
Parent Signature and Comments:			Teacher Comments:	

Figure 6.1 Number Systems Check Up

Name _____

Write in the numerals to represent the following statements. Be sure to add some of your own ideas in the open spaces provided.

	Roman	Chinese/ Japanese	Egyptian	Mayan	Babylonian	Arabic-Hindu
How old you are						
The number of people in your family, including yourself						
The number of eggs in a dozen						
The year in which you were born						
How old you are when you get a driver's license						
The number of pets you have						
The number of students in your class						

Some good resources and Web sites on number systems follow:

Number Systems

Can You Count Like a Greek? Exploring Ancient Number Systems, by Judy Leimbach and Kathy Leimbach

Writing Numbers

The Downs FM: Writing Numbers, www.teachingideas.co.uk/maths/numbersys.htm

Egyptian Numerals

Hieroglyphs, www.greatscott.com/hiero/index.html

Braille Web Site

Braille Bug, www.afb.org/braillebug/

Patterns and Sequencing

Patterns are found everywhere—they can be seen in fabrics, numbers, shapes, nature, and architecture. Looking for patterns within problems helps solve difficult tasks, and studying patterns helps students realize that finding and understanding patterns will help them become good problem solvers.

Problem	*Rule*
1, 3, 5, 7, 9, 11, <u>13</u>	Odd numbers
6, 5, 8, 7, 10, 9, <u>12</u>	Minus 1, plus 3, minus 1, plus 3, etc.
8, 4, 6, 2, 4, 0, <u>2</u>	Minus 4, plus 2, etc.
10, 8, 11, 7, 12, <u>6, 13</u>	Subtract 2, add 3, subtract 4, add 5, subtract 6, etc.
13, 26, 78, 312, <u>1560</u>	Multiply by 2, multiply by 3, multiply by 4, etc.
32, 40, 47, 53, 58, <u>62</u>	Add 8, add 7, add 6, etc.
29, 35, 47, 65, <u>89</u>	Add 6, add 12, add 18, add 24, etc.
41, 82, 84, 252, 255, <u>1020</u>	Multiply by 2, add 2, multiply by 3, add 3, etc.
49, 147, 150, 50, 47, 141, <u>144</u>	Multiply by 3, add 3, divide by 3, subtract 3, multiply by 3, etc.
28, 28, 27, 54, 52, 156, 153, <u>612</u>	Multiply by 1, subtract 1, multiply by 2, subtract 2, multiply by 3, etc.
58, 65, 70, 78, 82, 91, <u>94</u>	Add 7, add 5, add 8, add 4, add 9, add 3, etc.

I introduce patterns by having students give me examples of what patterns are and where they can be found. Then they solve various types of patterns, such as number, shape, and word patterns. Following are some number patterns that can be used orally in the classroom or on the board for a whole group discussion. The underlined numbers are the ones that the students should figure out.

SET Pattern Game

SET is a card game that reinforces pattern identification. This engaging game helps students understand relationships when searching for patterns. In order to make a set, students have to find three cards among the twelve cards laid out on the table that fit particular attributes in color, number, shading, and shape. The attributes in the set for each feature are either the same on each card or are different on each card. My students and I thoroughly enjoy playing this fast-paced pattern game. After playing this game numerous times, I noticed how well my students improved their analyzing skills and in identifying patterns. SET is a card game and there is also a daily game online at: www.setgame.com/set/puzzle_frame.htm. Students love the online game because it's a new game every day and the program times them on how long it takes them to find six sets. It is quick, challenging, and educational.

Other Pattern Information

A mathematician named Leonardo Fibonacci created a widely recognized number pattern called the Fibonacci sequence: 1, 1, 2, 3, 5, 8 . . . The rule for this pattern is that it starts with 1 and each number that follows is the sum of the previous two numbers ($1 + 1 = 2$, $1 + 2 = 3$, $2 + 3 = 5$, etc.). The Fibonacci number pattern "appears repeatedly in real, natural phenomena as diverse as pinecones and poems, sunflowers and symphonies, ancient art and modern computers, the solar system and the stock market" (Garland, 1987, p. 5). The Fibonacci number pattern is found in the growth pattern of plants. For example, the number of bracts in each round of the spiral on a pinecone is almost always one of the Fibonacci numbers.

Pattern Resources

Fascinating Fibonaccis: Mystery and Magic in Numbers, by Trudi Hammel Garland (1987)

By Nature's Design, by Pat Murphy (1993)

Easier Fibonacci Puzzles, www.mcs.surrey.ac.uk/Personal/R.Knott/ Fibonacci/fibpuzzles.html

Wollygoggles and Other Creatures: Problems for Developing Thinking Skills, by Thomas C. O'Brien (1980)

Mystery Numbers

Everyone loves a mystery! Getting students to solve a mystery improves their deductive and reasoning skills. This unit of study introduces students to math terms such as *product, factor, multiple, divisible, sum, difference, quotient, even, odd, less than,* and *greater than.* After these words are defined, students can solve puzzles with mystery numbers in groups or individually. I usually start them off with easy problems and then progress to more challenging puzzles. Try this easy puzzle.

> I am a two-digit number. I am an even number. When you add my digits together you get 5. I am less than 20. What number am I? (14)

For a culminating activity, students create their own mystery-number puzzle with ten clues. With older students, incorporate technology into this unit by having them type up their clues into a shape booklet. Using Microsoft PowerPoint, students select a shape in the drawing tools and draw this shape on half of the page. They then copy this shape onto the same page so that two identical shapes are on one page. They create three more pages identical to the first. The first shape, on page 1, is the title page; the second shape contains clues 1 through 5, the third shape contains clues 6 through 10, and the fourth shape asks, "What is the mystery number?" Shape 5 is the answer page and shape 6 is the "About the Author" page. After students finish typing, the book is cut out and is ready for others to solve the puzzle.

To incorporate a cross-curricular unit on mysteries, use *Mystery Festival* by Kevin Beals and Carolyn Willard (1994) to have students analyze and interpret evidence in the search for solutions. You may also enjoy *Logic Number Puzzles* by Wade H. Sherard III (1998).

M. C. Escher

A study of M. C. Escher's life and tessellations helps students realize that math is not always just about numbers. To start this unit of study, read *The Greedy Triangle* by Marilyn Burns (1995) and talk about polygons and their properties. This lays the foundation for delving into tessellations, symmetry, and the wonderful artist and mathematician M. C. Escher.

A tessellation is a repeated pattern that covers an entire flat plane without any holes, gaps, or overlaps. I play the video *The Fantastic World of M. C. Escher* by Michele Emmer (1998) to provide details about Escher's life, tessellations, and optical illusions. I have students design their own hand-drawn tessellation based on Escher's work. They then create a computer-generated tessellation using a software program called Tesselmania.

Following are easy directions for how to create a tessellation by hand:

> Draw a polygon on cardboard or heavy paper (preferably a square).

> Using your scissors, take a "nibble" out of the polygon between one corner and the next corner. A nibble refers to a design cut out of the cardboard.

You can do three things with this nibble:

Take the nibble and slide it down and tape it into place, which is called a translation.

Take the nibble and rotate it and tape it onto the next side, which is called a rotation.

Take the nibble and slide it down and then flip it over before taping it into place. This is called a glide-reflection.

You can then also take another nibble out of the other side of the polygon and repeat the same process described above.

This is the template to trace over and over again on a piece of paper.

Add details and color to your tessellation.

Escher Book, Video, and CD-ROM Resources

The Fantastic World of M. C. Escher (video), by Michele Emmer (1998)

Escher Interactive (CD-ROM), by Harry N. Abrams (1996)

M. C. Escher: 29 Master Prints, by Maurits Cornelis Escher (1983)

Tessellation Web Sites

World of Escher, www.worldofescher.com/contest

What Are Tessellations, CoolMath.com, www.coolmath.com/tesspag1.htm

Mathematical Games

Everybody loves to play games, and my students especially enjoy playing a variety of math games. Studying mathematical games, such as Nim, puts students' problem-solving skills to the test. Nim is one of the oldest mathematical strategy games and has many variations. Nim is a verb meaning "to take." Partners play this strategy game with materials that can be found around the house. The most challenging part of Nim is figuring out the winning strategy for each type of game. Nim addresses the concepts of numeration, patterns, problem solving, computation and data collection, display, and interpretation skills (Pfeiffer, 1998).

Before delving into this game, students need to know the difference between a game of chance and a game of strategy. A game of chance is a game that utilizes dice, spinners, cards, and questions, whereas a strategy game is one where the player develops a way to win. The essential rules of Nim are:

It is a two-player game

The rules establish a goal or target number

Players take turns removing or adding objects

The rules determine how many objects can be taken on one turn

The rules state how to win the game

No skipping turns

There is a winning strategy; Nim is not a game of chance

An example of a Nim game follows:

1. Collect objects such as coins, markers, or buttons.
2. Decide upon a number of objects to play with, such as sixteen objects.
3. Place the objects in a line on the table.
4. Player one picks up one or two objects at a time.
5. Player two picks up one or two objects at a time.
6. No skipping turns.
7. The winner is the player who takes the last one or two objects off the table.

After studying various versions of Nim, students create their own version based on the principles of NIM.

Resources and Web Sites for Nim

Creating Nim Games, by Sherron Pfeiffer (1998)

Nim Game, www.archimedes-lab.org/game_nim/nim.html

TacTix, http://thinks.com/java/tactix/tactix.htm

The All New & Improved Fruit Game, www.2020tech.com/fruit/index.html

Overhead Number Game

In the overhead number game, the creativity components of fluency, elaboration, and originality are used. To play this game, place number tiles on the overhead projector. Students try to use each number tile only once in a problem to create a true number equation. They can use any of the operators (+, −, ×, ÷) as many times as needed. To develop fluency, students should write as many problems as they can think of in a certain amount of time. The length of the problem doesn't matter. Using the same tiles, students next try to create the longest number equation by using as many tiles as possible; this strengthens the creativity components of elaboration and originality.

Miscellaneous Mathematical Activities

Magic Squares. Students enjoy using their problem-solving skills in trying to create magic squares. A magic square is a square that is divided into a grid; different numbers are placed in the grid so that every row, column, and both diagonals add up to the same sum.

Algorithms in Multiplication. Show students different ways to multiply, such as lattice multiplication, Napier's bones, and Ethiopian multiplication, so that they see other methods of solving problems.

Cartesian Coordinate Graphing. Students enjoy learning how to graph in the four quadrants, especially with negative numbers. I create a floor grid on paper that has the quadrants on it and then give students a point that they need to stand on. This way I can assess how well they understand this concept. Then I have the first student be a point on the grid and hold a string. The next student takes the rest of the string and stands where his or her point is. This process continues until the last person completes the string drawing of a shape or object. For a culminating project, students draw a picture on the graph paper and then record the plot points. These plot points are then given to other students to recreate the picture. I have also used Microsoft Excel with graphing capabilities to do this graphing on the computer. The students love using the computer for this concept.

Stock Market. A study of the stock market will give students knowledge of what a stock is, how and when to buy stock, how to calculate and analyze stocks, and knowledge of stock terminology, such as *share price* and *bear market*. A spreadsheet computer program, such as Microsoft Excel, can be used to calculate stock price for a period of time using formulas; it can also create a graph.

Study of Famous Mathematicians/Theories. Students may want to study famous mathematicians and the theories that made them famous. This is not part of their regular math curriculum. For example, students may want to study Pascal, Goldbach, Pythagoras, or Fibonacci.

7

Visual/Spatial Awareness

Students with strong visual/spatial awareness are able to see things in their mind and able to look at things from various angles. Armstrong (1994) states that this intelligence "involves sensitivity to color, line, shape, form, space, and the relationships that exist between these elements. It includes the capacity to visualize, to graphically represent visual or spatial ideas, and to orient oneself appropriately in a spatial matrix" (p. 2).

According to Armstrong (1994), some characteristics of individuals with these talents are:

- Liking the arts, such as painting, drawing, and sculpting
- Having a photogenic memory; seeing things in pictures
- Liking to read maps, graphs, and charts
- Enjoying doing jigsaw puzzles, mazes, and other visual puzzles
- Having a strong capacity to visualize a situation
- Tending to look at the "big picture"
- Daydreaming a great deal

John was a third grader who had difficulty taking notes and writing ideas down on paper. His teacher contacted me for some suggestions to help with his writing difficulties.

> ## John
>
> John would just sit and daydream in class when it came to many writing assignments, but when he had free time he enjoyed completing jigsaw puzzles and thrived at the art center. He loved incorporating a variety of art supplies, such as colors, fabric, and craft materials in an art project. To help remedy his writing difficulties, I had him do mind mapping when he took notes. Mind mapping is a technique where students can organize information using pictures, color, and words. John enjoyed using this technique to help organize his thoughts and ideas because he was a visual learner.

The following analysis activities are designed to test a student's visual/spatial awareness skills utilizing pentonimo pieces.

■ ANALYSIS ACTIVITIES

Activity 1: Pentominoes

Teacher Notes/Grading: Provide students with more than sixty small square pieces and graph paper to create pentomino pieces. A pentomino consists of five squares that are connected together by at least one common side. Remind students that if two shapes can be turned, flipped, or rotated to match, they are the same shape. There are twelve pentomino possibilities. Use the pentomino answer key as a reference guide. This activity assesses student's visual and spatial awareness. Students who can create nine or more pentomino pieces have good visual/spatial skills.

Directions:

Use the square pieces to create as many pentomino pieces that you can. A pentomino piece consists of five squares that are connected together and have at least one common side. The squares need to line up with other pieces; a piece can't straddle two other pieces—see the examples of incorrect pieces. Remember that if two shapes can be flipped, rotated, or turned to match, they are the same shape (see Figure 7.1). You can use the square pieces as a guide and use the graph paper to record your answers.

Figure 7.1 Examples of Non-Pentomino Pieces

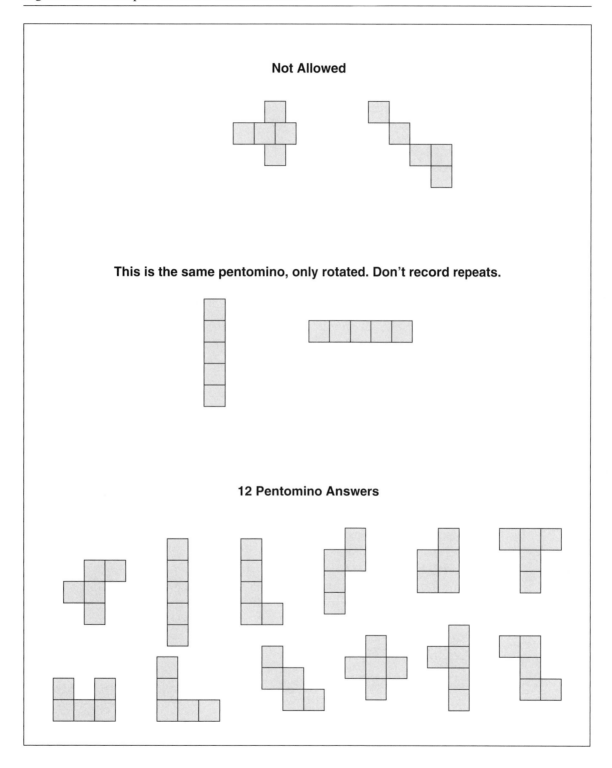

Activity 2: Pentomino Cards

Teacher Notes/Grading: Students use pentomino pieces to solve the puzzles. I recommend copying the pentomino sheet and laminating it before you cut the pieces out for the students so they will be more durable. Plastic pentomino pieces can be bought from a teacher's supply store or from teacher catalogs. Students with good visual/spatial skills should be able to complete two out of the three puzzles correctly. There may be more than one way to solve the puzzle.

Directions:

Using your pentomino pieces, cover the picture to solve it. There will be no gaps or overlapping pieces when you solve this puzzle. See Figure 7.2 for the puzzle pieces; use Figures 7.3, 7.5, and 7.7 for the actual puzzles. The answers to the puzzles are found in Figures 7.4, 7.6, and 7.8.

■ ENHANCING VISUAL/SPATIAL SKILLS

Students who are talented in the visual/spatial intelligence view the world, problems, and situations differently from others. They see things in images and pictures, can visualize things, and can recall placement of objects easily.

Tangram Puzzles

A tangram is an old Chinese puzzle that can be used to challenge gifted students. A tangram set includes seven shapes or pieces: five triangles, a square, and a parallelogram; each piece is called a "tan." I like to introduce this topic by reading the story *Grandfather Tang's Story: A Tale Told With Tangrams* by Ann Tompert (1990). This playful story introduces students to the use of tangrams. I then have students play with a set of tangrams to make various pictures on their own and have them use all seven pieces to make a square. After the children have had some experience with the puzzle pieces, I have them solve tangram puzzles. There are various books on tangram puzzle activities, and some of the puzzles I made up to challenge students are included in this chapter. For a culminating activity, students can create their own tangram puzzles for others to solve. Students can even use two sets of tangrams to create their puzzle. Tangrams can be viewed from problem-solving and creativity aspects, as well as visual/spatial. See Figure 7.9 for the puzzle pieces; use Figures 7.10, 7.12, 7.14, and 7.16 for the actual puzzles. The answers to the puzzles are found in Figures 7.11, 7.13, 7.15, and 7.17.

Tangram Resources

Tangram Patterns, by Thomas Foster (1977)

Tangram Puzzles: 500 Tricky Shapes to Confound & Astound, by Chris Crawford (2002)

Three Pigs, One Wolf, and Seven Magic Shapes, by Grace Maccarone and Marilyn Burns (1998)

(Text Continues on Page 96)

Figure 7.2

Pentomino Puzzle Pieces, Page 1

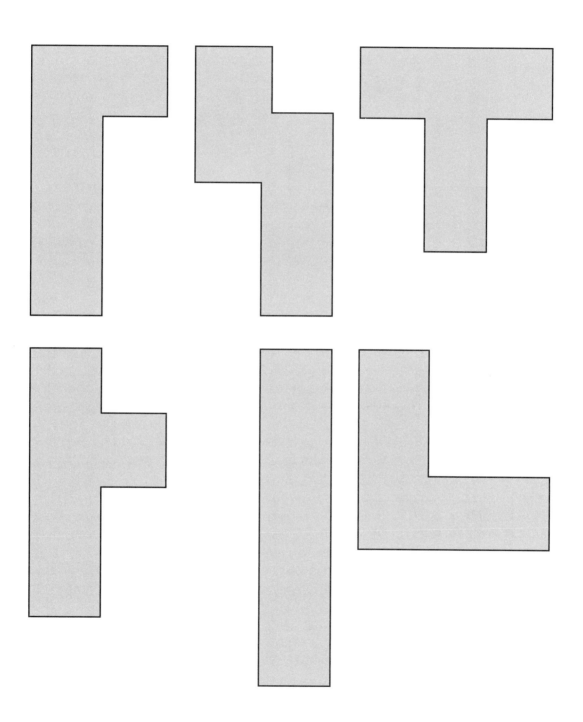

(Continued)

Figure 7.2 (Continued)

Pentomino Puzzle Pieces, Page 2

Figure 7.3

Pentomino Puzzle 1

Figure 7.4

Answer to Pentomino Puzzle 1

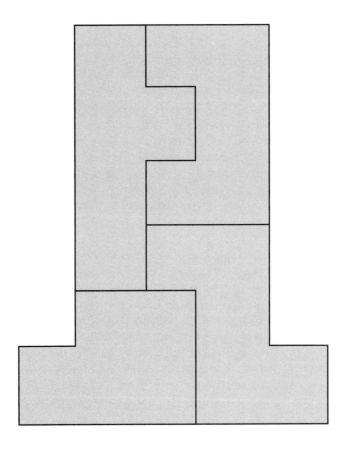

Figure 7.5

Pentomino Puzzle 2

Figure 7.6

Answer to Pentomino Puzzle 2

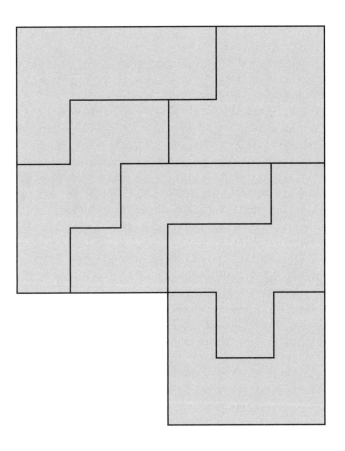

Figure 7.7

Pentomino Puzzle 3

Figure 7.8

Answer to Pentomino Puzzle 3

Figure 7.9

Tangram Puzzle Pieces

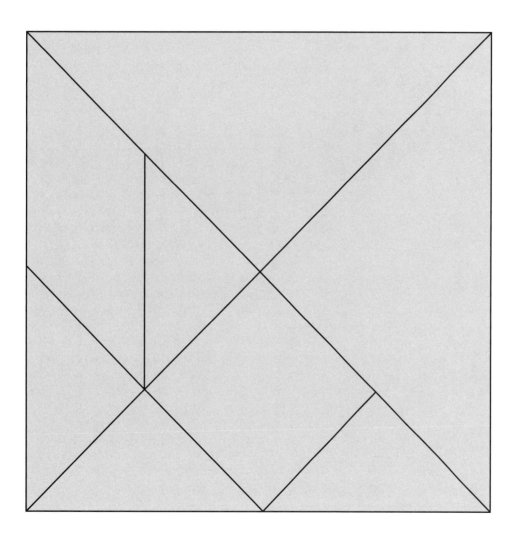

Figure 7.10

Tangram Card: Bird in Flight. With 5 tangram pieces, make this figure.

Bird in Flight

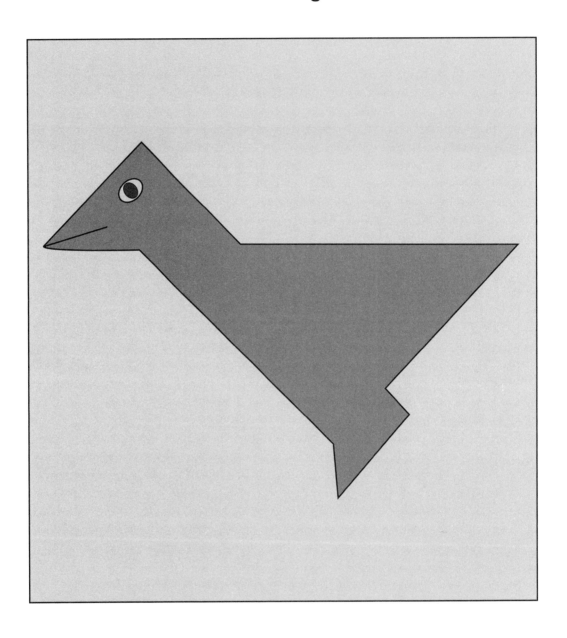

Figure 7.11

Solution to Tangram Card: Bird in Flight

Tangram Card

Bird in Flight

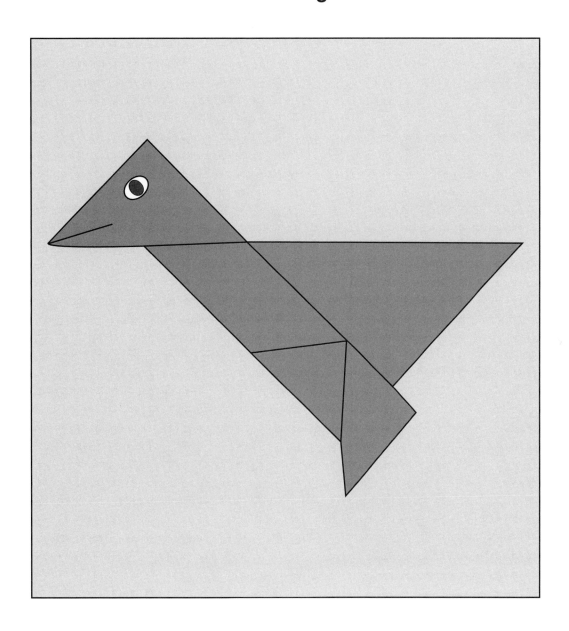

Figure 7.12

Tangram Card: Boy Kicking Ball.
With all 7 tangram pieces, make this figure.

Boy Kicking Ball

Figure 7.13

Solution to Tangram Card: Boy Kicking Ball

Tangram Card

Boy Kicking Ball

Figure 7.14

Tangram Card: Hot Air Balloon.
With all 7 tangram pieces, make this figure.

Hot Air Balloon

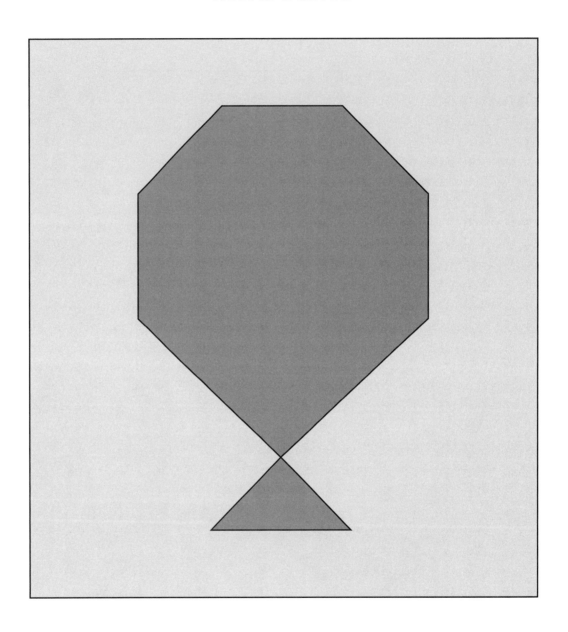

Figure 7.15

Solution to Tangram Card: Hot Air Balloon

Tangram Card

Hot Air Balloon

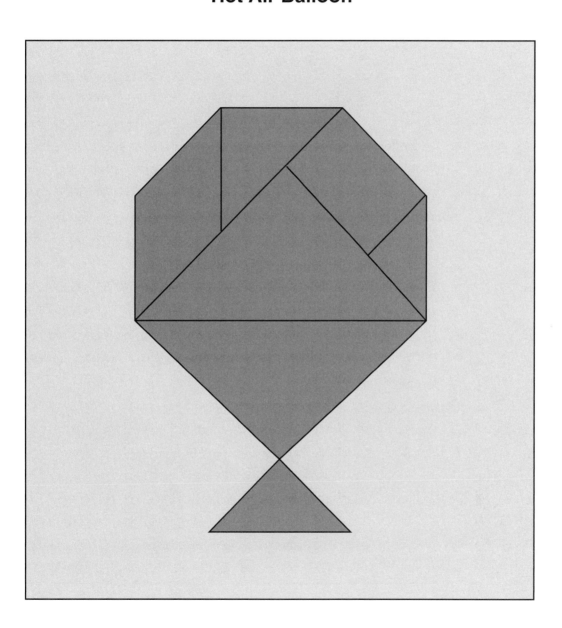

Figure 7.16

Tangram Card: Fish Looking at a Fishing Hook.
With all 7 tangram pieces, make this figure.

Fish Looking at a Fishing Hook

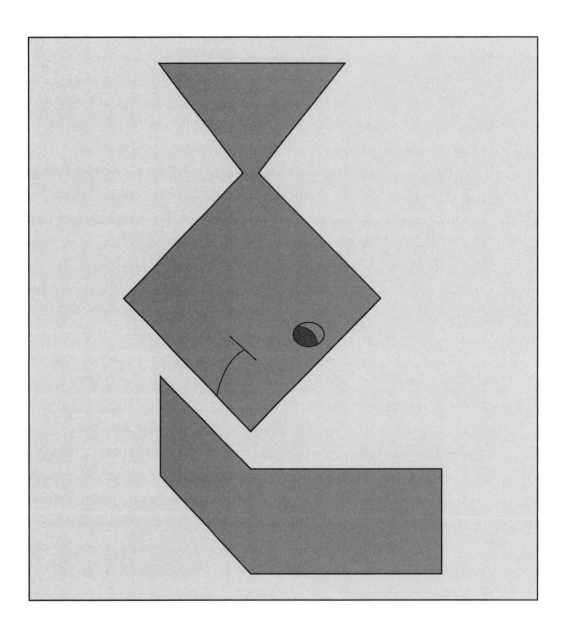

Figure 7.17

Solution to Tangram Card: Fish Looking at a Fishing Hook

Tangram

Fish Looking at a Fishing Hook

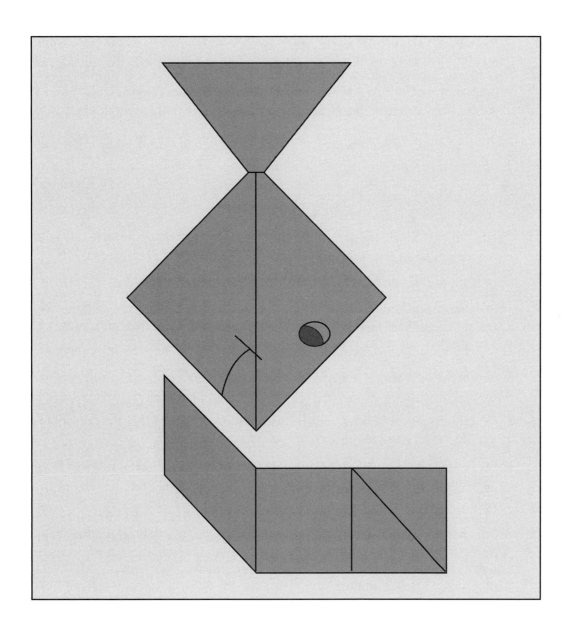

Mind Mapping

In the 1960s, Tony Buzan developed mind mapping to help teachers and students organize information quickly by using drawings or key words (see Buzan & Buzan, 1996). This technique is also useful for remembering and reviewing ideas. Mind maps can be used across the curriculum from brainstorming, writing, and note taking to problem solving.

Since the inception of mind mapping, there has been "increasing evidence that the ability to put thoughts into images as well as words enhances thinking skills and actually improves intelligence" (Margulies, 1991, p. 12). This technique of drawing images and using key words helps students remember things more easily because an image is very memorable. Some advantages of mind maps include the amount of information that can be put on a page, mind maps are easy to read, they are very fast to produce, they help analyze information that needs to be put into categories, they show connections between pieces of information, and the information is easier to use for review.

According to Margulies (1991), the key steps in mind mapping are as follows:

Start by drawing a picture or a word that depicts the topic in the center of the page and work outward.

Use key words or images. Remember, you don't need to be an artist— a quick sketch is fine.

Put key words on lines to reinforce the structure of notes.

Use various colors to represent themes and to make things stand out; anything that stands out on the page will stand out in your mind.

Use lines, arrows, or other marks to show links between different ideas.

If you can't think of any more ideas in one area, move to another area.

Put ideas down on the paper as fast as you think of them. Don't judge, criticize, or hold back ideas. It is okay to cross off ideas on your map. Messy is acceptable.

Break boundaries. If you run out of space, don't start a new sheet; tape more paper onto the map.

Mind mapping can be beneficial to all grade levels for a variety of subjects, but it is great for gifted students because their minds can sometimes think so fast that they can't write fast enough. Using colors and pictures may help them visualize their ideas better. Primary teachers can use mind mapping to help students organize their ideas for a story using pictures and words. Intermediate teachers can have students use this technique to review for a test, as a different way of note-taking, and as a way to organize ideas for writing assignments. Students enjoy mind mapping because it gives them a creative way to express their ideas with color and pictures instead of just words in a straight line.

There is software available by Inspiration that creates mind maps with words and pictures on the computer. There is also a KidsInspiration mind mapping software that is geared toward younger students. For more information on these software programs, go to www.inspiration.com. For more information on mind mapping, go to www.buzanworld.com/mindmaps.

Droodles

A droodle is a doodle and a riddle. These puzzles are pictures that can be viewed from different perspectives and do not have right or wrong answers. Students exercise their creativity skills with this activity and can create their own droodles for others to solve. See the example shown in Figure 7.18.

Figure 7.18   A Butterfly Climbing Up a Rope

A butterfly climbing up a rope

Droodle Resources Online

The Droodles Homepage, www.droodles.com

Exploratorium Exhibits: The Meaning of Droodles, www.exploratorium.edu/exhibits/droodles

Memory Glance Game

Cut a variety of unrelated pictures out of a magazine and paste them onto a sheet of paper. You could use computer graphics, instead, to make this easier. Let students study the piece of paper for two minutes. After two minutes, turn the paper over and have them recall as many of the objects that were on the page as possible. I discuss the strategies that the students used to help them memorize the objects. Some of the strategies that have worked for my students are creating a story that correlates with each of the objects, organizing the objects together by categories, or visualizing them in color and moving. You can also have the students keep a graph of their results to show improvement during the year. This is a quick and easy activity to do when you have some time between lessons.

This activity can also be done with an interesting picture with many details. After looking at the picture for two minutes, students talk about everything that they saw. You can pose questions about the picture, such as what time was on the clock, what color were the girl's clothes, or how many toys were on the floor. Check for students' recollection of details—with practice, it should improve dramatically.

Idea Drawing

Ask students to quickly sketch ideas on paper after they learn some new information to show their understanding. A discussion of how the drawing relates to the subject matter is a very important aspect of this technique. Their drawings should not be evaluated. "Teachers should recognize the value this kind of visual thinking can have in helping students articulate their understanding of subject matter" (Armstrong, 1994, p. 73). This technique can be used across the curriculum, from fractions to electricity.

Miscellaneous Visual/Spatial Ideas

Incorporate the Use of Graphs, Diagrams, and Charts Across the Curriculum. This can range from simple graphs of the number of students who order lunch, to more detailed history timelines. Use them as often as possible to help these students relate to the curriculum.

Create a Piece of Artwork, Collage, or Mural That You Weave Into Various Subject Areas. This activity can be used as a culminating project to show understanding of material instead of a written or oral report. Giving students the option for a final project helps students with strong intelligences to self-select an appropriate way to share their knowledge.

Work With Colors and Textures to Create a Piece of Artwork. Create a center where various art supplies, such as cloth, yarn, paper, markers, and buttons, are accessible for students to design a piece of artwork. The more variety in the types of supplies the better, because this gives visual/spatial students a means to excel and express themselves.

Put Together Jigsaw Puzzles of Various Kinds. Puzzles now even come in 3-D form—a project that these students will thoroughly enjoy.

Go on Field Trips to Museums. If you can't take a field trip, a museum can come to the classroom through virtual tours. The Metropolitan Museum of Art (www .metmuseum.org) and the Louvre (www.louvre.fr) are great Web sites to explore.

Delve Into Photography. Create a photography club and teach different aspects of the subject, such as perspective. Digital cameras are a great resource within the classroom for these students—for example, if your students are learning about personification in poetry, they can take pictures around the school. Then, using one of the pictures, they can personify the picture in their poem. They can also create a booklet of their photos and poems or make a PowerPoint presentation.

Try 3-D Construction Kits. There are various 3-D construction kits that can correlate with curriculum. For example, there is a bridge-building kit that relates to architecture, the study of the London Bridge, or transportation. Other 3-D puzzle kits include 3-D Problem Solving with Omnifix cubes (puzzles using Omnifix cubes that connect to create a model), 3-D pentomino puzzles, and Geosphere (creates a 3-D ball).

Teach Art Classes and Art Appreciation. These students love to work with color, shape, and form. Providing extensive opportunities for these students to excel in their strength area is very important. Studying famous artists as well as appreciating various types of art is beneficial to these children.

Use Visual Thinking. Have students close their eyes and picture what they are studying. Afterward, they can draw or talk about their experiences. This technique helps visual students recall information more easily.

Use Color Coding. Students can color-code notes or information for easier recall and understanding, such as using the color red for identifying the key points of something and using green to mark the supporting details. Color coding can be done in many subject areas.

Create a Slideshow on a Topic and Incorporate Graphics and Colors. A computer slideshow program such as Microsoft PowerPoint can be used in all subject areas. Graphics, colors, animation, and sound will enhance learning for these students.

Play Games. Various games that will exercise the visual/spatial intelligence are available at www.thinkfun.com; they include TipOver, Rush Hour, Block by Block, and Visual Brainstorms. The Web site also has games that can be played online. Other games that build upon the visual/spatial intelligence include: Time Blocks (you have one minute to recreate a picture using blocks), Rubics Cube, Squzzle Puzzles (using nine pieces, create a 3 × 3 puzzle), and Tangeos (recreate an image shown on a card using the pieces).

Mazes and Mysteries. Visual/Spatial learners like mazes, "I Spy," and "Where's Waldo?" books.

Optical Illusions. This is another area that these students will enjoy. There are various books available on the topic, such as *The Little Giant Book of Optical Illusions* by Keith Kay (1977) and *Visual Illusions* by Matthew Luckiesch and William H. Ittleson (1998).

Create Origami.

Additional Visual/Spatial Resource

Visual Thinking: Entertaining Activities to Increase Intelligence, by Marco Meirovitz and Paul I. Jacobs (1987)

8

Cross-Curricular Projects

The lesson and unit ideas in this chapter address cross-curricular topics of study with an emphasis on technology. Students tend to enjoy working on these because the lessons expose them to new information as well as help them develop technological skills that they will use in the future. After I demonstrate a new computer feature, students often tell me that they are working on a similar project at home, practicing these features. This is so important because they are applying what they learned to new situations and they are excited to learn new things.

The following projects incorporate many subject areas—every one of your students can find something here to be excited about, and each one of the activities will help gifted students improve upon their area of strength as well as challenge their other, weaker areas.

DESIGN YOUR OWN DREAM ROOM ■

In the dream room project, students draw scale models of their room on graph paper and on the computer, incorporating architecture elements, calculations, creative writing, and use of spreadsheets. This cross-curricular project incorporates language arts, mathematics, architecture, creativity components, oral presentation skills, and visual/spatial skills.

Students first brainstorm a list of things that they would like in their dream room if money were not an object. Using the size of my classroom as their dream room size, students work with partners to measure the classroom. They then must design blueprints of their new room, incorporating architectural elements drawn to scale on graph paper. I show the students how to scale the room to fit on a piece of paper. Then they transfer this blueprint onto the computer. I have used Microsoft Word for the scale drawing and set the gridlines feature on the screen for more accurate scale drawings. If a computer-aided design (CAD) program is available, it would work very nicely.

Next, students need to calculate the floor area of the room, figure out how much carpet is needed, and figure out how much it would cost. Utilizing Microsoft Excel, students calculate how much their dream room will cost them, including the price for each item (prices can't be made up), tax, and shipping and handling using formulas. A written description of the room and a creative addition round out this project. The creative addition can be a scale model, a video, picture book samples, or any other idea that deals with their dream room. After the projects are completed, students hone their oral presentation skills by sharing their rooms with the class.

Teacher Notes/Grading: Here are the requirements and a sample grading rubric that I have used with the Dream Room project. This rubric can be adapted for almost any activity in the book.

Project Dream Room

Phase One: Dream Room

1. Construct an aerial view of your dream room on graph paper, drawn to scale, including measurements of the room. Remember doors, windows, and electrical outlets. The room should be the size of the classroom, as measured in class.

2. Transfer your drawing of your dream room onto the computer and label the size of the room and each diagram or shape, using the architectural key sheet as a guide.

Phase Two: Carpet

Calculate the floor area in your new room. Suppose carpet will cost $25.98 a square yard. How much carpet will you need? How much will it cost?

Phase Three: Spreadsheet

Using the spreadsheet program on the computer, calculate how much money you spend to create this dream room. Record where each item is from, quantity, price, tax, shipping and handling, and the grand total for everything (using formulas).

If you want a leather sofa in your room, you need to find a store that sells that sofa and the cost. You may not make up prices for items—look in catalogs for actual prices. Don't forget about the prices of sheets, drapes, lamps, and other accessories that you want in your room.

Phase Four: Description

Write a detailed description of your dream room.

Phase Five: Creative Addition

Include some creative addition to your project that is not mentioned above. For example, create a drawing of how your house would look from the outside and include architecture elements, or create a scale model of your dream room, and so on.

Phase Six: Final Project

Include all the pages from the phases in an organized manner with a cover page.

Figure 8.1   Dream Room Descriptor

PARTS	Possible Points	Student Points	Teacher Points	ATTRIBUTES
Phase One	10			Aerial view of dream on graph paper drawn to scale. Measure and record size (use architectural key).
	5			Correct room measurements
	15			Computer drawing: accurate labels, correct spelling
Phase Two	5			Calculate the cost of the carpet in sq. yards (show work)
Phase Three	10			Spreadsheet of items to be bought—include store, item, quantity, price, tax, S/H, and grand total
Phase Four	10			Detailed written description
Phase Five	15			Personal creative addition to this project
Phase Six	5			Correct spelling and grammar
	5			Bind final project in your own style, such as a booklet format, in an organized way
	10			Creative ideas in the overall project
	5			Use of computer time wisely
	5			Being prepared (hand in on time)
Total	**100**			
Parent Signature and Comments:			Teacher Comments:	

■ CREATE A COMPANY AND AN ADVERTISEMENT

Students create a company that sells a product or provides a service. In this unit, students look at different types of companies, logo designs, and understand words such as *profit* and *consumer*. I arrange for a speaker to come in from the small business association to speak to the students about opening up their own business. Students brainstorm company ideas that would make their lives easier or better. They then web out ideas for a company saying, description of product or service, price, and location, and design their own logo. With this information, students design a computer-generated brochure or a catalog to advertise their company. They also design a business card for their company. Students create spreadsheets with formulas and graphs to track the company's profit, number of items sold, employee wages, and other business details. Many additional activities can be incorporated in this project, such as making a commercial or creating a jingle for the company. The computer software programs that I have used for this project are Microsoft Publisher and Microsoft Excel, but it is easy to add in a digital camera, a scanner, and other devices. Here is a sample of what I've given my students in the past:

Create a Company That Sells a Product or Provides a Service

Design a colorful and eye-catching brochure/catalog using the computer.

1. The advertisement for your company must include certain computer aspects. The following are the requirements for your project.

   Use graphics from the computer library.

   Create a logo for your company.

   Describe your product/service.

   Create a catchy saying for your product/service.

   Use a scanned image.

   Use the digital camera.

2. Create a computer-generated spreadsheet and graph using formulas. The graph should be completed using the spreadsheet. This may be used to keep a tally of the number of items sold, the total cost of each product, and so forth.

3. Design a business card. Include your logo, name, address, city, state, zip code, e-mail, and Web site address.

4. Creative Addition: Develop a creative addition for this project, such as a video, a prototype of the item or items your company sells, a map showing how you would display these items, or a map of your store.

Use your creativity with this project! There are many different ways that this project can be approached.

DESIGN A WEBQUEST   ■

A WebQuest is an inquiry-oriented activity in which some or all of the information that a learner interacts with comes from the Internet. In 1995, Bernie Dodge and Tom March from San Diego State University developed this model. WebQuests direct learners to Web sites to find research about a particular topic.

I have my students create their own WebQuest. The first step in creating a WebQuest is having students select their topic. I challenge students to select a topic that they don't know much about so that they can gain new knowledge. Students can also use a subject that they are passionate about for an independent study project for their WebQuest.

WebQuests have several parts: Introduction, Task, Process, Resources, Evaluation, and the Conclusion (see Figure 8.2).

The *Introduction page* piques the interest of the learner and encourages completing the WebQuest.

The *Task page*, a very important part of a WebQuest, describes what the students will do with the information they learn. Examples of tasks include making an oral report, giving a slideshow, or creating a brochure.

The *Process page* gives the student detailed directions or strategies on how to complete the task, such as, "Look up ten vocabulary words on hurricanes," "Include graphics with your ten-page slideshow," or "Use a word-processing software program to write a five-minute speech that you will share with the class."

The *Resource page* lists all the Web sites and books that students should use to complete the task.

The *Evaluation page* has the rubric that students will use to grade themselves on completing the task.

The *Conclusion page* brings closure to the WebQuest and states things for students to think about.

Using a word-processing program, students type all of the information for each part of the WebQuest. I have a premade word processing file for the students to use as their template. This allows them to add the detailed information for each part of the WebQuest without worrying about graphics and hyperlinks at this stage.

After they have completed the typing, I show students how to create their WebQuest using Microsoft Publisher, a very user-friendly Web-design program, but any Web-design program will work. Students then copy their information from the word-processing program into the Web-design program. They then hyperlink their Web sources and add graphics. When completed, students present their WebQuest to others, enhancing their communication skills.

WebQuest Online Resources

The WebQuest Page, http://webquest.sdsu.edu/

Eduscapes.com, www.educscapes.com/sessions/travel/36webquests.htm

TechTrekers: WebQuests, www.techtrekers.com/webquests/

Figure 8.2   Creating Your Own WebQuest

Your challenge is to design an interesting and informative WebQuest. Use graphics, hyperlinks, and color to make your WebQuest appealing for others to view and do.

Parts of a WebQuest

Introduction. Write a short paragraph to introduce the activity. This sets the stage and provides background information.

Task. Describe crisply and clearly what the end result of the learners' activities will be. This focuses learners on what they are going to do.
   The task can be a

- series of questions that must be answered
- summary to be created
- problem to be solved
- creative work
- position to be formulated and defended

Process. To accomplish the task, what steps should the learners go through? Number the steps. This outlines how the learners will accomplish the task.

Resources. This page points out places on the Internet or in books that will be available for the learners to use to accomplish the task.

Evaluation. This describes the evaluation criteria needed to meet performance and content standards. (Rubric)

Conclusion. This page summarizes what the learner will have accomplished or learned by completing this WebQuest. This brings closure and encourages reflection.

   On the bottom of the last page, write your name and how the learners can contact you with questions.

■ CREATE A SLIDESHOW PRESENTATION

Creating a slideshow presentation is useful in many areas of study. Topics can include a multimedia résumé, research on a famous person, poetry, independent study topic, and science experiment results. Learning the features of color, sound, animation, slide transitions, and the use of graphics helps students realize the importance of adding detail to a project. I have used Microsoft PowerPoint, which works well for this project.

INDEGENDENT STUDY ◼

Many students have a passion for a particular topic that is not always connected to the school curriculum. The students' passion can lend itself to an independent study project, allowing them to use their area of strength to study this area more deeply. Interest-based independent projects give the students ownership of their learning. "Authentic and relevant learning engages students in a process where they learn by using real-world experiences in an area of study they choose" (Cooper, 1997, p. 22). Students excel when researching in their area of interest; they become fully engaged in their learning. A nice feature of an independent study is that it can be done with all age levels.

Creating a contract with the student that details the project requirements is one of the first steps in a successful independent study. The contract should be agreed upon and signed by both the teacher and the student. Student input into the decision-making process about the contract, topic of study, and evaluation process increases motivation (Winebrenner, 2001). Important parts of the contract include the following:

Amount of time needed for the project

Special requirements, such as where the work will take place and the types of materials that will be used

The behavior the student should adhere to while pursuing research: working quietly while others are working, not disrupting teaching time with questions, and so forth

When and how the progress on the project will be shared; a daily log of work should be kept

The due date for the project (if applicable). The due date for the project can range from two weeks upward to whenever the findings are complete, which may take a full semester. Timelines may vary from student to student and depend upon the topic being researched.

Independent study projects are student-centered and incorporate many facets, such as problem-solving and creative-thinking skills. These projects should be long-range so students can fully investigate their area of interest. Creating an environment where students feel independent, successful, and in charge of their own learning is very beneficial to both student and teacher.

Independent Study Resource Book

Teaching Gifted Kids in the Regular Classroom, by Susan Winebrenner (2001)

CREATE INTERACTIVE COMPUTER GAMES USING HYPERLINKS ◼

With this project, students select an educational topic and use Microsoft PowerPoint to design an interactive game. They learn how to create hyperlinks within their project to show the correct answer or to return to any question answered incorrectly. Games like Jeopardy!, Who Wants to Be a Millionaire?, and matching games are popular games that are fairly easy to create. Following are some Web sites to help with this project.

Tech Teachers: Jeopardy Templates and Other Games, www.techteachers .com/jeopardytemplates.htm

PowerPoint Lessons, http://teach.fcps.net/trt10/PowerPoint.htm#temp

■ DESIGN A PIECE OF ARTWORK

Students design a piece of artwork or a CD cover after listening to a piece of music, such as something by Mozart. Using a computer drawing program such as Microsoft PhotoDraw, students draw what they feel or think the CD cover would look like. They can also incorporate writing into this project by describing their feelings, which can be put into a poem.

■ ALL ABOUT ME PROJECT

This project is a good way to start the beginning of the year and get to know your students better. Students answer questions about themselves, such as what they are good at, what they like to do in their free time, and their favorite subject in school. They use the Internet to find historic events that happened on their birthday, who shares their birthday, and what their name means. They also need to figure out how many hours old they are. Using a presentation program such as Microsoft PowerPoint, students use the "Autoshape" tool to create a shape on the page and type information inside the shape. Using hyperlinks, students link words to the Web sites that correlate with the information. Students can also use a digital camera to incorporate their picture in this project.

■ CREATE A DATABASE

A database project can be used with multiple topics or research options. I have used a database software program, such as Microsoft Access, to show students the important features of a database, such as how things can be sorted easily, how to create lists of selected information, or how to create mailing labels. Ideas for using a database can be as simple as an address book, a book list (author, character, and genre), state information, animal information (location, diet), or family genealogy.

■ DESIGN A TRAVEL BROCHURE

This lesson ties into the social studies curriculum and can be used for all grade levels. After studying a place in the world, students use Microsoft Publisher to create a travel brochure (one great thing about Publisher is that you can select the type of fold you want for your brochure). For example, students can create a travel brochure about the rain forest. They can type in information as well as use pictures to describe the features and locations of rain forests. This type of brochure can be used in a variety of ways from listing the features of community helpers to showing how things work.

CREATE A SQUIGGLE DRAWING ■

This is a quick partner project where one student draws a squiggly line on a page using Microsoft PowerPoint or any program that has line tools. The second person then uses this line as a base and extends the first line or adds new lines to it to create a drawing. The partners need to add details to their drawing. This activity can be done with very young students as well as older students, and is a good activity for visual/spatial learners. After a unit of study, you may want them to base this squiggly drawing procedure on something they just learned about.

HERO UNIT ■

A unit on heroes incorporates brainstorming, writing, creativity, research skills, and art. I first have students brainstorm all of the characteristics or qualities that make up a hero (see the section titled "Enhancing Creative-Thinking Skills" in Chapter 3 for brainstorming rules). As a class, the students create a list of real people or professional jobs that they feel exhibit the qualities of a hero.

I then have the students brainstorm a list of superheroes that they know of. We talk about their superpowers or talents, costumes, villains, sidekicks, secret identities, and hideouts. I have students list at least twenty adjectives that would describe a superhero and tell them these will be used later in their project. We then compare the list of qualities and characteristics of a real-life hero with those of superheroes. It can be helpful to use a Venn diagram for the comparison.

For culminating activity, students create their own superhero adventure story, incorporating all of the features that were researched and the superhero adjectives. Using a mind map or story map (see "Mind Mapping" in Chapter 7 for instructions), they plan out their superhero adventure story. If they like, they can make their story into a comic book, a pop-up book, or a book with illustrations. I let the students choose their final project option.

Add a creative flair to this project by having students design a model of their superhero. Students receive $200 of imaginary money (capital) to spend on designing their superhero. They need to buy a license; design and construct their superhero's outfit; buy, rent, sell, or barter for supplies; and enter the contest. Students keep a balance sheet where they add and deduct monetary amounts for items they buy, sell, rent, or barter. They will need to buy materials such as paper, markers, glue, and sequins to create their superhero model. After the students have designed their superhero, they are awarded money for their use of creative ideas and detailed descriptions. The ultimate goal is to be the one with the most capital at the end of the contest. Below is a sample of the introduction sheet I give my students.

The Superior Superhero

The Superior Superhero group needs a fresh supply of sensational, supreme, supercharged, superhumans! You have been offered the opportunity to do what all the computers could not do . . .

PRODUCE A SUPER-DUPER SUPERHERO!

You have been selected for your creativity, ingenuity, honor, and bravery and are invited to enter a design in the contest.

You will be given the sum of $200 with which to begin (this is called your working capital). The winner(s) of the contest will be the one that follows the rules and guidelines and increases his or her capital to end with the largest amount of money.

READY TO ACCEPT THE CHALLENGE? THEN LET'S GO!

1. Form a company and give it an exciting, creative name.

2. Begin your balance sheet with $200.

3. Buy a license (Designer Permission Slip) for $100. Deduct this amount from your balance sheet.

4. Purchase supplies.

5. Design and construct your superhero. Buy, rent, sell, and barter for supplies.

6. Enter the contest, keeping in mind that the superhero you create should
   • be creatively designed
   • possess the most original capabilities
   • be accompanied by written work
   • have "E.S.P"—Extra Special Products

BUT HOW CAN I EARN MONEY?

• Sell or rent supplies to other companies
• Write a detailed list of super things your hero can do or has accomplished
• E.S.P.: $100 each if judged worthy
• Original Items: $100 each if no other company has the same idea
• Use the following words correctly in relation to your superhero ($20 each): *saintly, scrawny, sapient, sequacious, sagacious, salient, salable, sallow, sarcastic, satirical, scholarly,* and *scrupulous*

Examples of Supplies:

SUPER STICK-EMS

Glue

Pins

Tape

Paperclips

Paper fasteners

COLOR-FULLS

Markers

Crayons

Colored pencils

CONSTRUCTABLES

Paper (all kinds)

Cardboard

MECHANICAL TOOLS

Scissors

Rulers

Pencils

Staplers

CREATIVE COLLECTION

Moveable eyes

Sequins

Ribbon

Other

THE RADIO SHOW ■

Challenge students to create a talk radio program that includes current events, news, music, and commercials. Play old recordings of famous radio programs to spark students' creativity. Students can work in groups or individually to develop a radio program. They should gear their program toward a certain age group. The Radio Lovers Web site has more information on famous radio programs and interesting radio broadcasts: www.radiolovers.com.

MY CREATIVE STATE ■

Using the outline of your state, students create a new picture; they can turn the drawing of the state around in any direction. Using this drawing,

Figure 8.3

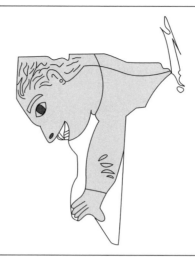

students create a story about their picture that includes factual information about their state. For example, some of my students interweave key items such as the state bird, flag, and bodies of water within their creative story. This lesson ties into the social studies curriculum very well, and adds a creative component to the generic topic of learning about their state. One example can be seen in Figure 8.3.

Conclusion

When working with gifted children, it is essential to inspire a zest for learning new things every day. The regular curriculum often bores them, as does the busywork they're generally given as a result of finishing tasks early. Spotting students' potential giftedness and providing the necessary educational opportunities is vital to creating this zest, and is the first step in helping them develop a lifelong love for learning.

My hope is that the units and activities in this book become catalysts for your gifted students, inspiring them to delve deeper into their favorite subjects and to use their talents to meet challenges head-on. The activities provided here can be changed and modified to meet the individual needs of your students, and I encourage you to play around with the various ideas and use them as springboards for discussions and independent projects. The ideas and possibilities are limitless! Select an idea and explore it in depth with your students; they will love the novel lesson ideas and ask for more, and you will help them become involved in their own learning.

It is not always easy to meet the needs of gifted students, but gaining insight into students' unique strengths and helping them grow into their potential is every educator's dream. This kind of growth in the classroom can also help: I have found that as a teacher of gifted children, my students have encouraged me to work harder and think more creatively in order to find new ways to challenge them. It truly is a win-win situation.

I hope that you have found these units and activities as useful as I have with my gifted students. If my history is any guide, your students will remember the special activities you have done with them for years to come and will apply the skills they learned to other areas of their lives. What more could a teacher ask for?

Good luck on the wonderful endeavor that lies ahead of you!

References

Abrams, H. N. (1996). *Escher interactive* (CD-ROM edition). New York: Harry N. Abrams.

Allen, R. (1997). *MENSA secret codes for kids.* New York: Scholastic.

Andreasen, N. (2005). *The creating brain: The neuroscience of genius.* Washington, DC: Dana Press.

Antonietti, A. (1997, March). Unlocking creativity. *Educational Leadership, 54*(6), 73–75.

Appelbaum, M., & Catanese, J. (2001). *Folk tale plays from around the world—That kids will love!* New York: Scholastic.

Armstrong, T. (1994). *Multiple intelligences in the classroom.* Alexandria, VA: Association for Supervision and Curriculum Development.

Beals, K., & Willard, C. (1994). *Mystery festival: Teacher's guide* (Great Explorations in Math and Science [GEMS] series). Berkeley: University of California, Lawrence Hall of Science.

Brandt, R. (1997, March). On using knowledge about our brain: A conversation with Bob Sylwester. *Educational Leadership, 54*(6), 16–19.

Brynildssen, S. (2000). *Vocabulary's influence on successful writing* (ERIC Digest No. D157). Bloomington, IN: ERIC Clearinghouse on Reading English and Communication. (Available online at http://www.ericdigests.org/2001-3/influence.htm)

Burns, M. (1995). *The greedy triangle* (Brainy Day Books series). New York: Scholastic.

Buzan, T., & Buzan, B. (1996). *Mind map book: How to use radiant thinking to maximize your brain's untapped potential.* New York: Penguin.

Caine, R., & Caine, G. (1991). *Making connections: Teaching and the human brain.* Alexandria, VA: Association for Supervision and Curriculum Development.

Cooper, C. R. (1997, September). When your child is way ahead: What your school should be doing. *Parenting for High Potential, 23.*

Costa, A. L. (1991). *Developing minds: A resource book for teaching thinking.* Alexandria, VA: Association for Supervision and Curriculum Development.

Cotton, K. (1991, November). *Teaching thinking skills.* Retrieved January 9, 2006, from http://www.nwrel.org/scpd/sirs/6/cu11.html

Crawford, C. (2002). *Tangram puzzles: 500 tricky shapes to confound & astound/Includes deluxe wood tangrams.* New York: Sterling Publishing.

Creative thinking: How to use de Bono's "Six thinking hats" to improve your thinking skills. (2005). Retrieved January 9, 2006, from http://www.buildingbrands.com/goodthinking/08_six_thinking_hats.shtml

Cullum, A. (1993). *Aesop's fables plays for young children.* Carthage, IL: Fearon Teacher Aides.

de Bono, E. (1991a). *Six thinking hats for schools: 3–5 resource book.* Logan, IA: Perfection Learning.

de Bono, E. (1991b). *Six thinking hats for schools: 6–8 resource book.* Logan, IA: Perfection Learning.

D'Arcangelo, M. (1998, November). The brains behind the brain. *Educational Leadership, 56*(3), 20–25.

Eberle, B. (1997a). *SCAMPER: Creative games and activities for imagination development.* Austin, TX: Prufrock Press.

Eberle, B. (1997b). *SCAMPER On: Creative games and activities for imagination development.* Austin, TX: Prufrock Press.

Emmer, M. (Director). (1998). *The fantastic world of M. C. Escher* [Video]. Silver Spring, MD: Acorn Media.

Escher, M. C. (1983). *M. C. Escher: 29 master prints.* New York: Harry N. Abrams.

Foltz Jones, C. (1991). *Mistakes that worked.* New York: Bantam Doubleday.

Foster, T. H. (1977). *Tangram patterns.* Palo Alto, CA: Creative Publications.

Gardner, H. (1983). *Frames of mind: The theory of multiple intelligences.* New York: Basic Books.

Gardner, H. (1991). *The unschooled mind: How children think and how schools should teach.* New York: Basic Books.

Garland, T. H. (1987). *Fascinating Fibonaccis: Mystery and magic in numbers.* Palo Alto, CA: Dale Seymour.

Harris, R. (1998). *Introduction to creative thinking.* Retrieved December 15, 2005, from http://www.virtualsalt.com/crebook1.htm

Howe, R., & Warren, C. R. (1989). Teaching critical thinking through environmental education. *ERIC/SMEAC Environmental Education Digest 2.* (Available online at http://ericae.net/edo/ed324193.htm)

Johnson, D. T. (2000). *Teaching mathematics to gifted students in a mixed-ability classroom* (ERIC EC Digest No. E594). Arlington, VA: ERIC Clearinghouse on Disabilities and Gifted Education. (Available online at http:// www.ericdigests.org/ 2001-1/math.html)

Kay, K. (1997). *The Little Giant book of optical illusions.* New York: Sterling Publishing.

Krensky, S. (2004). *There once was a very odd school: And other lunch-box limericks.* New York: Penguin Young Readers.

Leimbach, J. (2005). *Primarily logic.* Waco, TX: Prufrock Press.

Leimbach, J., & Leimbach, K. (1990). *Can you count like a Greek? Exploring ancient number systems.* San Luis Obispo, CA: Dandy Lion Publications.

Levy, N. (various). *Stories with holes* [Stories With Holes series]. Hightstown, NJ: N. L. Associates.

Levy, S. (1996). *Starting from scratch: One classroom builds its own curriculum.* Portsmouth, NH: Heinemann.

Luckiesch, M., & Ittleson, W. H. (1998). *Visual illusions.* Mineola, NY: Dover Publications.

Maccarone, G., & Burns, M. (1998). *Three pigs, one wolf, and seven magic shapes.* New York: Scholastic.

Maker, C. J., & Nielson, A. B. (1995). *Teaching models in education of the gifted* (2nd ed.). Austin, TX: Pro-Ed.

Margulies, N. (1991). *Mapping inner space: Learning and teaching mind mapping.* Tucson, AZ: Zephyr Press.

Meirovitz, M., & Jacobs, P. I. (1987). *Visual thinking: Entertaining activities to increase intelligence.* Monroe, NY: Trillium Press.

Miller, M. (1998). *Codemaster book #1: How to write and decode secret messages.* New York: Scholastic.

Miller, R. C. (1990). *Discovering mathematical talent* (ERIC EC Digest No. E482). Arlington, VA: ERIC Clearinghouse on Disabilities and Gifted Education. (Available online at http://www.ericdigests.org/1994/talent.htm)

Murphy, P. (1993). *By nature's design.* San Francisco: Chronicle Books.

O'Brien, E., & Riddell, D. (1997). *The Usborne book of secret codes.* New York: Scholastic.

O'Brien, T. C. (1980). *Wollygoggles and other creatures: Problems for developing thinking skills.* New Rochelle, NY: Cuisenaire Company of America.

Pfeiffer, S. (1998). *Creating Nim games* (Math Project Series). New York: Dale Seymour.

Reed, S., & Westberg, K. L. (2003). Implementing enrichment clusters in a multiage school: Perspectives from a principal and consultant. *Gifted Child Today, 26*(4).

Risby, B. (2001). *Analogies for the 21st century.* San Luis Obispo, CA: Dandy Lion Publications.

Risby, B. (2005). *Logic safari: Book 1.* Austin, TX: Prufrock Press.

Shannon, G. (1985). *Stories to solve: Folktales from around the world.* New York: Greenwillow Books.

Shannon, G. (1994). *Still more stories to solve: Fourteen folktales from around the world.* New York: Greenwillow Books.

Sherard, W. H., III. (1998). *Logic number puzzles.* New York: Dale Seymour.

6 + 1 trait writing—About. (2005). Retrieved August 26, 2006, from http:// www .nwrel.org/assessment/about.php?odelay=1&d=1

Smith, C. B. (1997). *Vocabulary instruction and reading comprehension* (ERIC Digest ED412506). Bloomington, IN: ERIC Clearinghouse on Reading English and Communication. (Available online at http://www.ericdigests.org/1998-1/ vocabulary.htm)

Smith, K. (2003). *Logic puzzles to bend your brain.* New York: Sterling Publishing.

Smutny, J. F. (2001, June). *Creative strategies for teaching language arts to gifted students (K–8)* (ERIC Digest No. E612). Arlington, VA: Eric Clearinghouse on Disabilities and Gifted Education. (Available online at http://ericec.org/ digests/e612.html or http://www.ericdigests.org/1998-1/vocabulary.htm)

Smutny, J. F., Walker, S. Y., & Meckstroth, E. A. (1997). *Teaching young gifted children in the regular classroom: Identifying, nurturing, and challenging ages 4–9.* Minneapolis, MN: Free Spirit Publishing.

Sudoku. (2005). Bath, UK: Parragon Publishing.

Terban, M. (1985). *Too hot to hoot: Funny palindrome riddles.* New York: Clarion.

Tompert, A. (1990). *Grandfather Tang's story: A tale told with tangrams.* New York: Knopf.

Torrance, E. P. (1979). *The search for satori and creativity.* Buffalo, NY: Creative Education Foundation.

Winebrenner, S. (2001). *Teaching gifted kids in the regular classroom.* Minneapolis, MN: Free Spirit.

Winebrenner, S., & Devlin, B. (1996). *Cluster grouping of gifted students: How to provide full-time service on a part-time budget* (ERIC EC Digest No. E538). Arlington, VA: ERIC Clearinghouse on Disabilities and Gifted Education. Arlington, VA. (Available online at www.hoagiesgifted.org/eric/e538.html)

Wolfe, M. F. (2000). *Rube Goldberg: Inventions.* New York: Simon & Schuster Adult Publishing Group.

Additional Reading

Abrohms, A. (1992). *Problem solving with pentominoes.* Vernon Hills, IL: Learning Resources.

Assouline, S., & Lupkowski-Shoplik, A. (2003). *Developing mathematical talent: A guide for challenging and educating gifted students.* Waco, TX: Prufrock Press.

Brain-based learning. (2001). Retrieved December 19, 2005, from http://www .funderstanding.com/brain_based_learning.cfm

Characteristics and behaviors of the gifted. (n.d.). Retrieved May 12, 2005, from the Rhode Island State Advisory Committee on Gifted and Talented Education: http://www.ri.net/gifted_talented/character.html

Chipongian, L. (2006). *What is "brain-based learning"?* Retrieved November 2, 2005, from http://www.brainconnection.com/topics/?main=fa/brain-based

Dickinson, D. (2001). Humor and the multiple intelligences. Retrieved November 14, 2005, from http://www.newhorizons.org/strategies/mi/dickinson_ humor_mi.htm

Diffily, D. (2002, Summer). Project-based learning: Meeting social studies standards and the needs of gifted learners. *Gifted Child Today, 25*(3), 1–9.

Eide, B., & Eide, F. (2004). Brains on fire: The multimodality of gifted thinkers. New Horizons for Learning. Retrieved January 9, 2006, from http://www .newhorizons.org/spneeds/gifted/eide.htm

Ennis, R. H. (1985). Goals for a critical thinking curriculum. In A. Costa (Ed.), *Developing minds: A resource book for teaching thinking.* Alexandria, VA: Association for Supervision and Curriculum Development.

Ennis, R. H. (1987). A taxonomy of critical thinking dispositions and abilities. In J. Baron & R. Sternberg (Eds.), *Teaching thinking skills: Theory and practice.* New York: Freeman.

Escher, M. C. (1996). *The graphic work.* Germany: Barnes and Noble.

Giesecke, E. H. (1996). *3-D pentomino activity book.* Vernon Hills, IL: Learning Resources.

Haury, D. (1999). Mathematics education for gifted and talented children: How to recognize giftedness in mathematics. *The Eric Review, 6*(2), 48–49.

Johnsen, S. K. (2004). *Identifying gifted students: A practical guide.* Waco, TX: Prufrock Press.

Labelle, S. (2005). *Six thinking hats.* Retrieved January 9, 2006, from http://members .optusnet.com.au/~charles57/Creative/Techniques/sixhats.htm

Marzano, R. J., Brandt, R. S., Hughes, C. S., Jones, B. F., Presseisen, B. Z., Rankin, S. C., et al. (1988). *Dimensions of thinking: A framework for curriculum and instruction.* Alexandria, VA: Association for Supervision and Curriculum Development.

Multiple intelligence inventory: Eight styles of learning. (2001). Learning Disabilities Resource Community. Retrieved December 19, 2005, from http://www.ldrc .ca/projects/miinventory/miinventory.php?eightstyles=1

Parke, B. N. (1992, December). Challenging gifted students in the regular classroom (ERIC Digest E513). Retrieved January 3, 2007, from http://www.ericdigests.org/1993/gifted.htm

Perkins, D. N. (1984). Creativity by design. *Educational Leadership, 42*(1), 18–24.

Pool, C. R. (1997, March). Maximizing learning: A conversation with Renate Nummela Caine. *Educational Leadership, 54*(6), 11–15.

Risby, B. (2005). *Thinking through analogies.* Austin, TX: Prufrock Press.

Resnick, L. B., & Klopfer, L. E. (1989). *Toward the thinking curriculum: Current cognitive research.* Alexandria, VA: Association for Supervision and Curriculum Development.

Scriven, M., & Paul, R. (2004). *Defining critical thinking.* Retrieved January 9, 2006, from http://www.criticalthinking.org/aboutCT/definingCT.shtml

Starr, L. (2000). *Creating a WebQuest: It's easier than you think.* Retrieved December 19, 2005, from http://www.educationworld.com/a_tech/tech/tech011.shtml

Storm Fink, L. (2002). *Comics in the classroom as an introduction to genre study.* Retrieved January 9, 2006, from http://www.readwritethink.org/lessons/lesson_view.asp?id=188

Sylwester, R. (2005, December). *Connecting brain processes to school policies and practices.* Retrieved January 3, 2007, from http://www.brainconnection.com/content/224_1

Versaci, R. (2001). *How comic books can change the way our students see literature: One teacher's perspective.* Retrieved January 9, 2006, from http://www.teachingcomics.org/curriculum/perspective.php

Winebrenner, S., & Berger, S. (1999, Summer). Providing curriculum alternatives to motivate gifted students. *AGATE Newsletter,* pp. 24–26.